PERSPECTIVES ON

NEW MEDIA

UNIVERSITY WRITING

3RD EDITION

BYU ACADEM
PUBLISHIN(

NOTE OF CONTENT AND PERMISSIONS

All articles were printed by permission or under fair use.

Contents

SPIRITUAL PERSPECTIVES

Sharing the Gospel Using the Internet 3
  M. Russell Ballard

Things as They Really Are 9
  David A. Bednar

To Sweep the Earth as with a Flood. 23
  David A. Bednar

EDUCATION

Online Literacy Is a Lesser Kind 37
  Mark Bauerlein

Dear Students: Don't Let College Unplug Your Future. 43
  Gideon Burton

Teaching to the Text Message 53
  Andy Selsberg

How Computers Change the Way We Think. 55
  Sherry Turkle

Why the Smart Reading Device of the Future May Be ... Paper 62
  Brandon Keim

The Real Revolution in Online Education Isn't MOOCs . . . 67
  Michelle Weise

A Social Network Can Be a Learning Network 71
  Derek Bruff

They Loved Your G.P.A. Then They Saw Your Tweets. 75
  Natasha Singer

Why Free Is Not the Future of Digital Content in Education . 79
   Mary Cullinane

Why Free Online Classes Are Still the Future of Education . . 81
   Issie Lapowsky

POLITICS

Is Google Making Us Stupid? 87
   Nicholas Carr

Small Change: Why the Revolution Will Not Be Tweeted . . 97
   Malcolm Gladwell

Why Malcolm Gladwell Should Apologize to Social Media . . 108
   Edward Lee

The Political Power of Social Media 112
   Clay Shirky

Why 'Slacktivism' Matters 126
   Shannon Fisher

Slacktivism: The Downfall of Millennials 129
   Charlotte Robertson

RELATIONSHIPS

Don't Dismiss Online Relationships as Fantasy 135
   Regina Lynn

Rude People, Not Tech, Cause Bad Manners 138
   Regina Lynn

You Have No Friends 141
   Farhad Manjoo

Are We Facebook Friends Yet? 146
   Micah McArthur

Why I Don't Watch What My Kids Are Doing Online 148
   Jody Allard

Bubbles Carry a Lot of Weight 151
   Jessica Bennett

Contents

This Is How to Stalk Your Teenage Children Online 154
   Belinda Luscombe

Re: Our Relationship 156
   Emma Pierson

DIGITAL CULTURE

The Amorality of Web 2.0 163
   Nicholas Carr

The People Formerly Known as the Audience 169
   Jay Rosen

When My Kids Unplugged 172
   Susan Maushart

I Tweet, Therefore I Am 176
   Peggy Orenstein

The Myth of Multitasking 179
   Christine Rosen

Spotify Doesn't Hurt Artists:
My Band Would Be Nowhere Without It 185
   Ben Berry

#TheDress and the Rise of Attention-Policing 190
   Megan Garber

Welcome to the New Reputation Economy 194
   Rachel Botsman

Bibliography 205

Spiritual
Perspectives

Sharing the Gospel Using the Internet

M. RUSSELL BALLARD

I am in my 80th year. By some accounts that makes me pretty old. Actually, some folks think some of the Brethren may be too old to know what's going on in your world. Let me assure you we are very much aware.

A CHANGING WORLD

In the span of nearly 80 years, I've seen many changes. When I began my mission in England in 1948, the most common way for people to get news was through newspapers and radio.

How different the world is today. For many of you, if you read newspapers, the chances are you read them on the Internet. Ours is the world of cyberspace, cell phones that capture video, video and music downloads, social networks, text messaging and blogs, handhelds and podcasts.

This is the world of the future, with inventions undreamed of that will come in your lifetime as they have in mine. How will you use these marvelous inventions? More to the point, how will you use them to further the work of the Lord?

You have a great opportunity to be a powerful force for good in the Church and in the world. There is truth in the old adage that "the pen is mightier than the sword."[1] In many cases it is with words that you will accomplish the great things that you set out to do. And it's principally about ways to share those words that I want to talk to you.

From its beginnings, The Church of Jesus Christ of Latter-day Saints has used the power of the printed word to spread the message of the restored gospel throughout the world. The Lord, over the centuries, has

---

1 Edward Bulwer-Lytton, Richelieu (1839), act 2, scene 2; in John Bartlett, comp., Familiar Quotations, 14th ed. (1968), 601.

Ballard, M. Russell. "Sharing the Gospel Using the Internet." Commencement address at BYU-Hawaii, 15 Dec. 2007. *Ensign.* July 2008. Web. 5 Apr. 2011. © Intellectual Reserve, Inc.

had a hand in inspiring people to invent tools that facilitate the spreading of the gospel. The Church has adopted and embraced those tools, including print, broadcast media, and the Internet.

There are perhaps few inventions that have had a greater impact on the world than the printing press, invented by the inspired Johannes Gutenberg around 1436. The printing press enabled knowledge, including that contained in the Holy Bible, to be shared more widely than ever before.

THE INTERNET: A MODERN PRINTING PRESS

Today we have a modern equivalent of the printing press in the Internet. The Internet allows everyone to be a publisher, to have his or her voice heard, and it is revolutionizing society. Before the Internet there were great barriers to printing. It took money, power, influence, and a great amount of time to publish. But today, because of the emergence of what some call "new media," made possible by the Internet, many of those barriers have been removed. New media consists of tools on the Internet that make it possible for nearly anyone to publish or broadcast to either a large or a niche audience. I have mentioned some of these tools already. The emergence of new media is facilitating a worldwide conversation on almost every subject, including religion, and nearly everyone can participate. This modern equivalent of the printing press is not reserved only for the elite.

Now some of these tools—like any tool in an unpracticed or undisciplined hand—can be dangerous. The Internet can be used to proclaim the gospel of Jesus Christ and can just as easily be used to market the filth and sleaze of pornography. Computer applications like iTunes can be used to download uplifting and stirring music or the worst kind of antisocial lyrics full of profanity. Social networks on the Web can be used to expand healthy friendships as easily as they can be used by predators trying to trap the unwary. That is no different from how people choose to use television or movies or even a library. Satan is always quick to exploit the negative power of new inventions, to spoil and degrade, and to neutralize any effect for good. Make sure that the choices you make in the use of new media are choices that expand your mind, increase your opportunities, and feed your soul.

As you know, the new media has already profoundly impacted the old world of newspapers and other traditional media. Once upon a time, as a Church leader I might give a newspaper interview, then wait a day or two for it to appear somewhere deep inside the newspaper. Then that newspaper was thrown away, and whatever impact it might have had dissipated rather quickly.

Now, as I am leaving one appointment to go to the next, the report of my visit or interview begins almost immediately to appear on the newspaper's Web site or on blogs, where it can be copied and distributed all over the Web. You can see how important the right *words* are today. Words recorded on the Internet do not disappear. Any Google or Yahoo! search is going to find one's words, probably for a very long time.

A case in point: In 2007, NBC television came to Salt Lake for an interview with me as part of a piece they were producing on the Church. Reporter Ron Allen and I spent an hour together in the chapel in the Joseph Smith Memorial Building. We discussed the Church at length. A few days later the story appeared, and in the four-minute segment that aired, there was one short quote of about six seconds from the one-hour interview. That was just enough time for me to testify of our faith in Jesus Christ as the center of all we believe. I repeat, just six seconds were used from a 60-minute interview. Those six seconds are quite typical, actually, for members of the traditional TV media, who think and air in sound bites. The big difference from the old days to today is that the reporter also ran 15 minutes of our interview on the *NBC Nightly News* Web site. And those 15 minutes are still there. What we say is no longer on and off the screen in a flash, but it remains as part of a permanent archive and can appear on other sites that reuse the content. People using Internet search engines to hunt for topics about the Church will come across that interview and many others.

These tools allow organizations and individuals to completely bypass the news media and publish or broadcast their messages in their entirety to the intended audiences. For instance, last year the Church Public Affairs Department conducted an interview with Elder Dallin H. Oaks of the Quorum of the Twelve Apostles and Elder Lance B. Wickman of the Seventy regarding the Church's position on same-gender attraction. In the old days, to communicate our message to the public on an issue like this we would have had to rely on the news media. But this probing interview was conducted by Church Public Affairs staff and posted in its entirety on the Church's Web site, unfiltered by the news media.

JOINING THE CONVERSATION

There are conversations going on about the Church constantly. Those conversations will continue whether or not we choose to participate in them. But we cannot stand on the sidelines while others, including our critics, attempt to define what the Church teaches. While some conversations have audiences in the thousands or even millions, most are much, much smaller. But all conversations have an impact on those who participate in them. Perceptions of the Church are established one conversation at a time.

The challenge is that there are too many people participating in conversations about the Church for our Church personnel to converse with and respond to individually. We cannot answer every question, satisfy every inquiry, and respond to every inaccuracy that exists. We need to remember that there is a difference between interest and mere curiosity. Sometimes people just want to know what the Church is. And some who seek answers want them to come directly from a member of the Church. They appreciate one-on-one conversation.

All of you know that members of The Church of Jesus Christ of Latter-day Saints are reminded and encouraged continually to share the gospel with others. The Church is always looking for the most effective ways to declare its message. Preaching the gospel of the Restoration has always been special to me. I loved being a missionary in England. I loved being a mission president in Canada. And I love my present calling, which allows me opportunities to share the message of the Restoration of the gospel to the world and to testify that God the Father and His Son, Jesus Christ, appeared to the Prophet Joseph Smith in 1820. Through Joseph, the gospel that Jesus established in New Testament times was brought back. It had been lost with the deaths of the Apostles of old. I can share with the world the knowledge that priesthood authority, the doctrine, and the ordinances of the New Testament Church are once again on the earth. This is the most important work that we can participate in.

Now, may I ask that you join the conversation by participating on the Internet to share the gospel and to explain in simple and clear terms the message of the Restoration. Most of you already know that if you have access to the Internet you can start a blog in minutes and begin sharing what you know to be true. You can download videos from Church and other appropriate sites, including newsroom.lds.org, and send them to your friends. You can write to media sites on the Internet that report on the Church and voice your views as to the accuracy of the reports. *This, of course, requires that you understand the basic principles of the gospel.* It is essential that you are able to offer a clear and correct witness of gospel truths. It is also important that you and the people to whom you testify understand that you do not speak for the Church as a whole. You speak as one member—but you testify of the truths you have come to know.

Far too many people have a poor understanding of the Church because most of the information they hear about us is from news media reports that are often driven by controversies. Too much attention to controversy has a negative impact on peoples' perceptions of what The Church of Jesus Christ of Latter-day Saints really is.

Recently a columnist writing in a major U.S. newspaper was irresponsibly inaccurate in his description of the Church and our beliefs and practices. Dozens, perhaps even hundreds, of Church members and others who understand our beliefs commented on the newspaper's Web site, correcting the misconceptions he was spreading and calling for accuracy.

EXAMPLES OF WHAT YOU CAN DO

Let me give you a few other examples of how Church members are using the new media.

A Church member living in the Midwest of the United States makes a concerted effort to share the gospel every day, in person. He then writes a blog about his daily endeavors to share the teachings of the Book of Mormon and to give pass-along cards to all he meets. His effort to share the gospel so diligently is admirable, and his further effort to write about it no doubt inspires many others to do the same.

Others have recorded and posted their testimonies of the Restoration, the teachings of the Book of Mormon, and other gospel subjects on popular video-sharing sites. You too can tell your story to nonmembers in this way. Use stories and words that they will understand. Talk honestly and sincerely about the impact the gospel has had in your life, about how it has helped you overcome weaknesses or challenges and helped define your values. The audiences for these and other new media tools may often be small, but the cumulative effect of thousands of such stories can be great. The combined effort is certainly worth the outcome if but a few are influenced by your words of faith and love of God and His Son, Jesus Christ.

The Restoration of the gospel of Jesus Christ has no doubt had a powerful impact on your life. It has, in part, shaped who you are and what your future will be. Do not be afraid to share with others your experiences as a follower of the Lord Jesus Christ. We all have interesting stories that have influenced our identity. Sharing those stories is a nonthreatening way to talk to others. Telling those stories can help demystify the Church. You could help overcome misperceptions through your own sphere of influence, which ought to include the Internet.

THINGS TO AVOID

Every disciple of Christ will be most effective and do the most good by adopting a demeanor worthy of a follower of the Savior. Discussions focused on questioning, debating, and doubting gospel principles do little to build the kingdom of God. The Apostle Paul has admonished us to not be "ashamed of the gospel of Christ: for it is the power of God unto salvation" (Romans 1:16). Let us all stand firmly and speak with faith in sharing our message with the world. Many of you are returned missionaries and can carry on a meaningful conversation in the language you learned on your mission. Your outreach can be international.

As you participate in this conversation and utilize the tools of new media, remember who you are—Latter-day Saints. Remember, as the proverb states, that "a soft answer turneth away wrath: but grievous words stir up anger" (Proverbs 15:1). And remember that contention is of the devil (see 3 Nephi 11:29). There is no need to argue or contend with others regarding our beliefs. There is no need to become defensive or belligerent. Our position is solid; the Church is true. We simply need to have a conversation, as friends in the same room would have, always guided by the prompting of the Spirit and constantly remembering the Atonement of the Lord Jesus Christ, which reminds us of how precious are the children of our Father in Heaven.

May the Lord bless each of you that you will have a powerful influence on those you come in contact with. As I said in the beginning, the power of words is incredible. Let your voice be heard in this great cause of the gospel of Jesus Christ.

Things as They Really Are

DAVID A. BEDNAR

Brothers and sisters, I love you and am grateful to be with you. I extend a special welcome to those of you in your final year of seminary who are attending a CES broadcast for the first time. As you continue your education, I encourage you to take full advantage of the opportunities you will have to learn and grow spiritually by enrolling in and actively participating in institute classes. You also will be able to attend future CES firesides, which will strengthen and bless you.

As I have looked forward to and prepared for this opportunity to learn with you, I have come to better understand the strong feelings of Jacob, the brother of Nephi. He said, "I this day am weighed down with much ... desire and anxiety for the welfare of your souls" (Jacob 2:3). The message I want to share with you today has over time distilled upon my soul "as the dews from heaven" (D&C 121:45). I invite your earnest attention to a serious subject that has both immediate and eternal implications. I pray for the Holy Ghost to be with and teach each of us during our time together.

I long have been impressed with the simple and clear definition of truth set forth in the Book of Mormon: "The Spirit speaketh the truth and lieth not. Wherefore, it speaketh of things as they really are, and of things as they really will be; wherefore, these things are manifested unto us plainly, for the salvation of our souls" (Jacob 4:13; see also D&C 93:24).

Tonight we will focus upon the first major element of truth identified in this verse: "things as they really are." We first will review several key elements of our Heavenly Father's plan of happiness as the doctrinal foundation for knowing and understanding things as they really are. We then will consider methods of attack used by the adversary to distract us from or inhibit our capacity to discern things as they really are. And finally, we will discuss the responsibilities that rest upon you as the rising generation.

Bednar, David A. "Things as They Really Are." CES fireside for Young Adults. Rexburg, Idaho. 3 May 2009. ©2011 Intellectual Reserve, Inc.

You will need to be obedient, to honor sacred covenants, and to discern things consistently as they really are in today's world that grows ever more confused and wicked.

OUR DIVINE DESTINY

In "The Family: A Proclamation to the World," the First Presidency and Council of the Twelve Apostles declare that as spirit sons and daughters of God we "accepted His plan by which His children could obtain a physical body and gain earthly experience to progress toward perfection and ultimately realize [our] divine destiny as heirs of eternal life" ("The Family: A Proclamation to the World," *Ensign,* Nov. 1995, 102; or *Liahona,* Oct. 2004, 49). Please note the primary importance of obtaining a physical body in the process of progressing toward our divine destiny.

The Prophet Joseph Smith taught with clarity the importance of our physical bodies:

"We came to this earth that we might have a body and present it pure before God in the celestial kingdom. The great principle of happiness consists in having a body. The devil has no body, and herein is his punishment. He is pleased when he can obtain the tabernacle of man, and when cast out by the Savior he asked to go into the herd of swine, showing that he would prefer a swine's body to having none. All beings who have bodies have power over those who have not. The devil has no power over us only as we permit him; the moment we revolt at anything which comes from God, the devil takes power."[1]

Our physical bodies make possible a breadth, a depth, and an intensity of experience that simply could not be obtained in our premortal estate. President Boyd K. Packer has taught, "Our spirit and our body are combined in such a way that our body becomes an instrument of our mind and the foundation of our character."[2] Thus, our relationships with other people, our capacity to recognize and act in accordance with truth, and our ability to obey the principles and ordinances of the gospel of Jesus Christ are amplified through our physical bodies. In the classroom of mortality, we experience tenderness, love, kindness, happiness, sorrow, disappointment, pain, and even the challenges of physical limitations in ways that prepare us for eternity. Simply stated, there are lessons we must learn and experiences we must have, as the scriptures describe, "according to the flesh" (see 1 Nephi 19:6; Alma 7:12—13).

Apostles and prophets consistently have taught the mortal and eternal importance of our bodies. Paul declared:

"Know ye not that ye are the temple of God, and that the Spirit of God dwelleth in you?

"If any man defile the temple of God, him shall God destroy; for the temple of God is holy, which temple ye are" (1 Corinthians 3:16—17).

And in this dispensation the Lord revealed that "the spirit and the body are the soul of man" (D&C 88:15). A truth that really is and always will be is that the body and the spirit constitute our reality and identity. When body and spirit are inseparably connected, we can receive a fulness of joy; when they are separated, we cannot receive a fulness of joy (see D&C 93:33—34).

The Father's plan is designed to provide direction for His children, to help them become happy, and to bring them safely home to Him with resurrected, exalted bodies. Lucifer labors to make the sons and daughters of God confused and unhappy and to hinder their eternal progression. The overarching intent of the father of lies is that all of us would become "miserable like unto himself" (2 Nephi 2:27), and he works to distort the elements of the Father's plan he hates the most.

Satan does not have a body, and his eternal progress has been halted. Just as water flowing in a riverbed is stopped by a dam, so the adversary's eternal progress is thwarted because he does not have a physical body. Because of his rebellion, Lucifer has denied himself all of the mortal blessings and experiences made possible through a tabernacle of flesh and bones. He cannot learn the lessons that only an embodied spirit can learn. He cannot marry or enjoy the blessings of procreation and family life. He cannot abide the reality of a literal and universal resurrection of all mankind. One of the potent scriptural meanings of the word *damned* is illustrated in his inability to continue developing and becoming like our Heavenly Father.

Because a physical body is so central to the Father's plan of happiness and our spiritual development, we should not be surprised that Lucifer seeks to frustrate our progression by tempting us to use our bodies improperly. One of the ultimate ironies of eternity is that the adversary, who is miserable precisely because he has no physical body, invites and entices us to share in his misery through the improper use of our bodies. The very tool he does not have and cannot use is thus the primary target of his attempts to lure us to physical and spiritual destruction.

THE ADVERSARY'S ATTACKS

The adversary attempts to influence us both to misuse our physical bodies and to minimize the importance of our bodies. These two methods of attack are important for us to recognize and to repel.

When any of Heavenly Father's children misuse their physical tabernacles by violating the law of chastity, by using drugs and addictive substances, by disfiguring or defacing themselves, or by worshipping the false idol of body image, whether their own or that of others, Satan is delighted. To those of us who know and understand the plan of salvation, any defiling of the body is rebellion (see Mosiah 2:36—37; D&C 64:34—35) and a denial of our true identity as sons and daughters of God.

Now brothers and sisters, I cannot tell you all the ways whereby you may misuse your bodies, "for there are divers ways and means, even so many that I cannot number them" (Mosiah 4:29). You know what is right and what is wrong, and you have the individual responsibility to learn for yourself "by study and also by faith" (D&C 88:118) the things you should and should not do and the doctrinal reasons why you should and should not do those things. I testify that as you desire to so learn, as you "watch yourselves, and your thoughts, and your words, and your deeds, and observe the commandments of God, and continue in the faith of what ye have heard concerning the coming of our Lord, even unto the end of your lives" (Mosiah 4:30), you will be spiritually enlightened and protected. And according to your faithfulness and diligence, you will have the power to discern the deception and repel the attacks of the adversary as he tempts you to misuse your physical body.

Satan also strives to entice the sons and daughters of God to minimize the importance of their physical bodies. This particular type of attack is most subtle and diabolical. I want to provide several examples of how the adversary can pacify and lull us away into a sense of carnal security (see 2 Nephi 28:21) and encourage us to put at risk the earthly learning experiences that caused us to shout for joy (see Job 38:7) in the premortal existence.

For example, all of us can find enjoyment in a wide range of wholesome, entertaining, and engaging activities. But we diminish the importance of our bodies and jeopardize our physical well-being by going to unusual and dangerous extremes searching for an ever greater and more exhilarating adrenaline "rush." We may rationalize that surely nothing is wrong with such seemingly innocent exploits and adventures. However, putting at risk the very instrument God has given us to receive the learning experiences of mortality—merely to pursue a thrill or some supposed fun, to bolster ego, or to gain acceptance—truly minimizes the importance of our physical bodies.

Sadly, some young men and women in the Church today ignore "things as they really are" and neglect eternal relationships for digital distractions, diversions, and detours that have no lasting value. My heart aches when a young couple—sealed together in the house of the Lord for time and for all eternity by the power of the holy priesthood—experiences marital difficulties because of the addicting effect of excessive video gaming or online socializing. A young man or woman may waste countless hours, postpone or forfeit vocational or academic achievement, and ultimately sacrifice cherished human relationships because of mind- and spirit-numbing video and online games. As the Lord declared, "Wherefore, I give unto them a commandment ... : Thou shalt not idle away thy time, neither shalt thou bury thy talent that it may not be known" (D&C 60:13).

You may now be asking yourself, "But Brother Bednar, you began today by talking about the importance of a physical body in our eternal progression. Are you suggesting that video gaming and various types of computer-mediated communication can play a role in minimizing the importance of our physical bodies?" That is precisely what I am declaring. Let me explain.

We live at a time when technology can be used to replicate reality, to augment reality, and to create virtual reality. For example, a medical doctor can use software simulation to gain valuable experience performing a complicated surgical operation without ever putting a human patient at risk. A pilot in a flight simulator repeatedly can practice emergency landing procedures that could save many lives. And architects and engineers can use innovative technologies to model sophisticated design and construction methods that decrease the loss of human life and damage to buildings caused by earthquakes and other natural disasters.

In each of these examples, a high degree of fidelity in the simulation or model contributes to the effectiveness of the experience. The term *fidelity* denotes the similarity between reality and a representation of reality. Such a simulation can be constructive if the fidelity is high and the purposes are good—for example, providing experience that saves lives or improves the quality of life.

The image shown on the following page is a computer-generated rendering of a sealing room in the Newport Beach California Temple.

Rendering

This and similar images are used as part of the planning and design process for each new temple that is constructed. The rendering portrays fabrics, furnishings, fixtures, lighting, scale, and proportion to show how each component will look and feel when finished. In essence, the entire temple and all of its elements are designed in detail before construction ever begins.

This picture is an actual photograph of the sealing room in the Newport Beach California Temple.

Photo

Please notice the fidelity between the representation of reality in the rendering (first image) and the reality of the completed room in this photograph.

This next image is a computer-generated rendering of a lobby area in the Copenhagen Denmark Temple.

Rendering

The following photo is the actual lobby in the Copenhagen Denmark Temple.

Photo

In each of these examples, high fidelity is employed to accomplish a most important purpose—the design and construction of a sacred and beautiful temple. However, a simulation or model can lead to spiritual impairment and danger if the fidelity is high and the purposes are bad—such as experimenting with actions contrary to God's commandments or enticing us to think or do things we would not otherwise think or do "because it is only a game."

Today I raise an apostolic voice of warning about the potentially stifling, suffocating, suppressing, and constraining impact of some kinds of cyberspace interactions and experiences upon our souls. The concerns I raise are not new; they apply equally to other types of media, such as television, movies, and music. But in a cyber world, these challenges are more pervasive and intense. I plead with you to beware of the sense-dulling and spiritually destructive influence of cyberspace technologies that are used to produce high fidelity and that promote degrading and evil purposes.

If the adversary cannot entice us to misuse our physical bodies, then one of his most potent tactics is to beguile you and me as embodied spirits to disconnect gradually and physically from things as they really are. In essence, he encourages us to think and act as if we were in our premortal, unembodied state. And, if we let him, he can cunningly employ some aspects of modern technology to accomplish his purposes. Please be careful of becoming so immersed and engrossed in pixels, texting, ear buds, twittering, online social networking, and potentially addictive uses of media and the Internet that you fail to recognize the importance of your physical body and miss the richness of person-to-person communication. Beware of digital displays and data in many forms of computer-mediated interaction that can displace the full range of physical capacity and experience.

Listen carefully to the following quote describing an intense romantic relationship a woman had with a cyberspace boyfriend. And note how the medium of communication minimized the importance of the physical body. "And so PFSlider [the man's screen name] became my everyday life. All the tangible stuff fell away. My body did not exist. I had no skin, no hair, no bones. All desire had converted itself into a cerebral current that reached nothing but my frontal lobe. There was no outdoors, no social life, no weather. There was only the computer screen and the phone, my chair, and maybe a glass of water."[3]

In contrast, we need to heed the admonition of Paul: "That every one of you should know how to possess his vessel in sanctification and honour" (1 Thessalonians 4:4).

Consider again the example I mentioned earlier of a young couple recently married in the house of the Lord. An immature or misguided spouse may devote an inordinate amount of time to playing video games, chatting online, or in other ways allowing the digital to dominate things as they really are. Initially the investment of time may seem relatively harmless, rationalized as a few minutes of needed relief from the demands of a hectic daily schedule. But important opportunities are missed for developing and improving interpersonal skills, for laughing and crying together, and for creating a rich and enduring bond of emotional intimacy. Progressively, seemingly innocent entertainment can become a form of pernicious enslavement.

To feel the warmth of a tender hug from an eternal companion or to see the sincerity in the eyes of another person as testimony is shared—all of these things experienced as they really are through the instrument of our physical body—could be sacrificed for a high fidelity fantasy that has no lasting value. If you and I are not vigilant, we can become "past feeling" (1 Nephi 17:45), as did Laman and Lemuel long ago.

Let me provide another example of disconnecting gradually and physically from things as they really are. Today a person can enter into a virtual world, such as Second Life, and assume a new identity. An individual can create an avatar, or a cyberspace persona, that conforms to his or her own appearance and behavior. Or a person can concoct a counterfeit identity that does not correlate in any way to things as they really are. However closely the assumed new identity approximates the individual, such behavior is the essence of things as they really are not. Earlier I defined the fidelity of a simulation or model. I now emphasize the importance of personal fidelity—the correspondence between an actual person and an assumed, cyberspace identity. Please note the lack of personal fidelity in the following episode as reported in the *Wall Street Journal:*

Ric Hoogestraat is "a burly [53-year-old] man with a long gray ponytail, thick sideburns and a salt-and-pepper handlebar mustache. ... [Ric spends] six hours a night and often 14 hours at a stretch on weekends as Dutch Hoorenbeek, his six-foot-nine, muscular ... cyber-self. The character looks like a younger, physically enhanced version of [Ric]."

"[He] sits at his computer with the blinds drawn. ... While his wife, Sue, watches television in the living room, Mr. Hoogestraat chats online with what appears on the screen to be a tall, slim redhead.

"He's never met the woman outside of the computer world of Second Life, a well-chronicled digital fantasyland. ... He's never so much as spoken to her on the telephone. But their relationship has taken on curiously real dimensions. They own two dogs, pay a mortgage together and spend hours [in their cyberspace world] shopping at the mall and taking long motorcycle rides. ... Their bond is so strong that three months ago, Mr. Hoogestraat asked Janet Spielman, the 38-year-old Canadian woman who controls the redhead, to become his virtual wife.

"The woman he's legally wed to is not amused. 'It's really devastating,' says Sue Hoogestraat, ... who has been married to Mr. Hoogestraat for seven months."[4]

Brothers and sisters, please understand. I am not suggesting all technology is inherently bad; it is not. Nor am I saying we should not use its many capabilities in appropriate ways to learn, to communicate, to lift and brighten lives, and to build and strengthen the Church; of course we should. But I am raising a warning voice that we should not squander and damage authentic relationships by obsessing over contrived ones. "Nearly 40% of men and 53% of women who play online games said their virtual friends were equal to or better than their real-life friends, according to a survey of 30,000 gamers conducted by ... a recent Ph.D. graduate from Stanford University. More than a quarter of gamers [who responded indicated that] the emotional highlight of the past week occurred in a computer world."[5]

How important, how enduring, and how timely is the Lord's definition of truth—"things as they really are." The prophet Alma asked, "O then, is not this real?" (Alma 32:35). He was speaking of light and good so discernible they can be tasted. Indeed, "they who dwell in [the Father's] presence ... see as they are seen, and know as they are known, having received of his fulness and of his grace" (D&C 76:94).

My beloved brothers and sisters, beware! To the extent personal fidelity decreases in computer-mediated communications and the purposes of such communications are distorted, perverted, and wicked, the potential for spiritual disaster is dangerously high. I implore you to turn away immediately and permanently from such places and activities (see 2 Timothy 3:5).

Now I would like to address an additional characteristic of the adversary's attacks. Satan often offers an alluring illusion of anonymity. Lucifer always has sought to accomplish his work in secret (see Moses 5:30). Remember, however, that apostasy is not anonymous simply because it occurs in a blog or through a fabricated identity in a chat room or virtual world. Immoral thoughts, words, and deeds always are immoral, even in cyberspace. Deceitful acts supposedly veiled in secrecy, such as illegally downloading music from the Internet or copying CDs or DVDs for distribution to friends and families, are nonetheless deceitful. We are all accountable to God, and ultimately we will be judged of Him according to our deeds and the desires of our hearts (see Alma 41:3). "For as [a man] thinketh in his heart, so is he" (Proverbs 23:7).

The Lord knows who we really are, what we really think, what we really do, and who we really are becoming. He has warned us that "the rebellious shall be pierced with much sorrow; for their iniquities shall be spoken upon the housetops, and their secret acts shall be revealed" (D&C 1:3).

I have raised a voice of warning about only a few of the spiritual hazards in our technologically oriented and rapidly changing world. Let me say again: neither technology nor rapid change in or of itself is good or evil; the real challenge is to understand both within the context of the eternal plan of happiness. Lucifer will encourage you to misuse and to minimize the importance of your physical body. He will attempt to substitute the monotony of virtual repetition for the infinite variety of God's creations and convince us we are merely mortal things to be acted upon instead of eternal souls blessed with moral agency to act for ourselves. Deviously, he entices embodied spirits to forfeit the blessings and learning experiences "according to the flesh" that are made possible through the Father's plan of happiness and the Atonement of His Only Begotten Son.

For your happiness and protection, I invite you to study more diligently the doctrine of the plan of salvation—and to prayerfully ponder the truths we have reviewed. I offer two questions for consideration in your personal pondering and prayerful studying:

1. Does the use of various technologies and media invite or impede the constant companionship of the Holy Ghost in your life?

2. Does the time you spend using various technologies and media enlarge or restrict your capacity to live, to love, and to serve in meaningful ways?

You will receive answers, inspiration, and instruction from the Holy Ghost suited to your individual circumstances and needs. I repeat and affirm the teaching of the Prophet Joseph: "All beings who have bodies have power over those who have not. The devil has no power over us only as we permit him."[6]

These eternal truths about the importance of our physical bodies will fortify you against the deception and the attacks of the adversary. One of my deepest desires for you is an ever-increasing testimony of and appreciation for the Resurrection—even your own resurrection with a celestial, exalted body "because of your faith in [the Lord Jesus Christ] according to the promise" (Moroni 7:41).

THE RISING GENERATION

I would like to speak specifically to you as you really are. You really are the rising generation in The Church of Jesus Christ of Latter-day Saints. In October of 1997, Elder Neal A. Maxwell visited the campus of Brigham Young University—Idaho to speak in a devotional. During the day he was on the campus, we talked together about a variety of gospel topics in general and about the youth of the Church in particular. I remember Elder Maxwell making a statement that greatly impressed me. He said, "The youth of this generation have a greater capacity for obedience than any previous generation."

He then indicated that his statement was based upon a truth taught by President George Q. Cannon: "God has reserved spirits for this dispensation who have the courage and determination to face the world, and all the powers of the evil one, visible and invisible, to proclaim the Gospel, and maintain the truth, and establish and build up the Zion of our God, fearless of all consequences. He has sent these spirits in this generation to lay the foundation of Zion never more to be overthrown, and to raise up a seed that will be righteous, and that will honor God, and honor him supremely, and be obedient to him under all circumstances."[7]

Parents and Church leaders frequently emphasize that the young men and women of this generation have been reserved for this season in the history of the world and are some of the most valiant of Heavenly Father's children. Indeed, such statements are true. But I often have wondered if young people hear this description so often that it becomes overused and trite—and that its importance and deep implications may be overlooked. We know that "unto whom much is given much is required" (D&C 82:3). And the teachings of President Cannon and Elder Maxwell help us to understand more fully what is required of us today. You and I are to be valiant and "obedient to him under all circumstances." Thus, obedience is the principal weapon upon which the rising generation must rely in the latter-day battle between good and evil.

We rejoice that the Lord through His authorized servants has "raised the bar" for the young men and women of today. Given what we know about who we are and why we are here upon the earth, such inspired direction is welcomed and appreciated. And we should recognize that Lucifer incessantly strives to "lower the bar" by coaxing us to misuse and minimize the importance of our physical bodies.

The Savior has warned us repeatedly to beware of deception by the adversary:

"Jesus answered, and said unto them: Take heed that no man deceive you; ...

"For in those days there shall also arise false Christs, and false prophets, and shall show great signs and wonders, insomuch, that, if possible, they shall deceive the very elect, who are the elect according to the covenant. ...

"And whoso treasureth up my word, shall not be deceived" (Joseph Smith—Matthew 1:5, 22, 37).

Obedience opens the door to the constant companionship of the Holy Ghost. And the spiritual gifts and abilities activated by the power of the Holy Ghost enable us to avoid deception—and to see, to feel, to know, to understand, and to remember things as they really are. You and I have been endowed with a greater capacity for obedience precisely for these reasons. Moroni declared:

"Hearken unto the words of the Lord, and ask the Father in the name of Jesus for what things soever ye shall stand in need. Doubt not, but be believing, and begin as in times of old, and come unto the Lord with all your heart, and work out your own salvation with fear and trembling before him.

"Be wise in the days of your probation; strip yourselves of all uncleanness; ask not, that ye may consume it on your lusts, but ask with a firmness unshaken, that ye will yield to no temptation, but that ye will serve the true and living God" (Mormon 9:27—28).

As we heed that inspired counsel, we can and will be blessed to recognize and repel the attacks of the adversary—today and in the days that lie ahead. We can and will fulfill our foreordained responsibilities and contribute to the work of the Lord in all the world.

I testify that God lives and is our Heavenly Father. He is the Author of the plan of salvation. Jesus is the Christ, the Redeemer, whose body was bruised, broken, and torn for us as He offered the atoning sacrifice. He is resurrected; He lives; and He stands at the head of His Church in these latter days. To be "encircled about eternally in the arms of his love" (2 Nephi 1:15) will be a real and not a virtual experience.

I testify we can and will be blessed with the courage and determination to face the world and all the powers of the evil one. Righteousness will prevail. No unhallowed hand can stop this work from progressing. I bear witness and testify of these things as they really are and as they really will be in the sacred name of the Lord Jesus Christ, amen.

NOTES

1. Quoted by William Clayton, reporting an undated discourse given by Joseph Smith in Nauvoo, Illinois; in L. John Nuttall, "Extracts from William Clayton's Private Book," 7—8, Journals of L. John Nuttall, 1857—1904, L. Tom Perry Special Collections, Brigham Young University, Provo, Utah; copy in Church History Library; spelling and capitalization standardized; see also *Teachings of Presidents of the Church: Joseph Smith* (2007), 211, 214.

2. Boyd K. Packer, *The Instrument of Your Mind and the Foundation of Your Character* (Church Educational System fireside for young adults, Feb. 2, 2003), 2.

3. Meghan Daum, "Virtual Love," *The New Yorker,* Aug. 25 and Sept. 1, 1997, 82; or Meghan Daum, *My Misspent Youth* (2001), 19.

4. Alexandra Alter, "Is This Man Cheating on His Wife?" *Wall Street Journal,* Aug. 10, 2007, W8, W1.

5. Alexandra Alter, *Wall Street Journal,* Aug. 10, 2007, W8.

6. Quoted by William Clayton; in L. John Nuttall, "Extracts from William Clayton's Private Book," 8.

7. George Q. Cannon, in *Journal of Discourses,* 11:230.

To Sweep the Earth as with a Flood

DAVID A. BEDNAR

Sister Bednar and I are grateful to worship together with you in this Brigham Young University Education Week devotional.

In 2009 I delivered a message to the young adults of the Church entitled "Things as They Really Are" and discussed the spiritual potential and pitfalls of various technologies in our modern world (see *Ensign*, June 2010, 16–25). My remarks today build upon and extend that previous message by focusing upon three related and important topics: (1) the unique season in the history of the world in which we live, even "the dispensation of the fulness of times," (2) the inspired technological and communication innovations that have come forth in this decisive dispensation, and (3) how we appropriately use these powerful tools to advance the work of salvation in all of the world.

I pray the Holy Ghost will teach and edify each of us as we consider together true principles and how to apply those principles in our lives.

THE DISPENSATION IN WHICH WE LIVE

We live in a truly distinctive dispensation.

A gospel dispensation is a period of time in which the necessary priesthood authority, ordinances, and doctrinal knowledge are found on the earth to implement the Father's plan of salvation for His children. Essential to the establishment of a dispensation is an authorized servant of God, a dispensation head, who holds and exercises the authority and keys of the holy priesthood. Gospel dispensations were established through Adam, Enoch, Noah, Abraham, Moses, Jesus Christ, Joseph Smith, and others. In every dispensation gospel truths are revealed anew—or dispensed—so the people of that period are not entirely dependent upon past dispensations for knowledge of Heavenly Father's plan.

Bednar, David A. "To Sweep the Earth as with a Flood." Education Week. BYU. 19 Aug. 2014. © Intellectual Reserve, Inc.

Apostasy from the truth occurred in each previous dispensation. However, the work of salvation that was commenced but not completed in those earlier eras continues into the final dispensation. The Prophet Joseph Smith explained that for this reason, the rolling forward of the latter-day glory, even the dispensation of the fulness of times, "is a cause that has interested the people of God in every age; it is a theme upon which prophets, priests and kings have dwelt with peculiar delight; they have looked forward with joyful anticipation to the day in which we live; and fired with heavenly and joyful anticipations they have sung and written and prophesied of this our day" (*Teachings of Presidents of the Church: Joseph Smith* [2007], 186).

In this greatest and last of all gospel dispensations, "a whole and complete and perfect union, and welding together of dispensations, and keys, and powers, and glories should take place, and be revealed from the days of Adam even to the present time. And not only this, but those things which have never been revealed from the foundation of the world, but have been kept hid from the wise and the prudent, shall be revealed ... in this, the dispensation of the fulness of times" (D&C 128:18).

The Prophet Joseph further expounded: "All the ordinances and duties that ever have been required by the Priesthood, under the directions and commandments of the Almighty in any of the dispensations, shall all be had in the last dispensation ... , bringing to pass the restoration spoken of by the mouth of all the Holy Prophets" (*Teachings: Joseph Smith,* 511).

As the Apostle Paul declared, "In the dispensation of the fulness of times [God will] gather together in one all things in Christ, both which are in heaven, and which are on earth; even in him" (Ephesians 1:10).

THE DISPENSATION OF THE FULNESS OF TIMES AND TECHNOLOGY

We are blessed to live, learn, and serve in this most remarkable dispensation. An important aspect of the fulness that is available to us in this special season is a miraculous progression of innovations and inventions that have enabled and accelerated the work of salvation: from trains to telegraphs to radios to automobiles to airplanes to telephones to transistors to televisions to computers to satellite transmissions to the Internet—and to an almost endless list of technologies and tools that bless our lives. All of these advancements are part of the Lord hastening His work in the latter days.

In 1862 Brigham Young said: "Every discovery in science and art, that is really true and useful to mankind has been given by direct revelation from God, though but few acknowledge it. It has been given with a view to prepare the way for the ultimate triumph of truth, and the redemption of the earth from the power of sin and Satan. We should take advantage of all these great discoveries, the accumulated wisdom of ages, and give to our children the benefit of every branch of useful knowledge, to prepare them to step forward and efficiently do their part in the great work" (*Discourses of Brigham Young,* sel. John A. Widtsoe [1954], 18–19).

In 1966 President David O. McKay prophesied scientific discoveries that "stagger the imagination" would make possible the preaching of the gospel to every kindred, tongue, and people. And further:

"Discoveries latent with such potent power, either for the blessing or the destruction of human beings, as to make man's responsibility in controlling them the most gigantic ever placed in human hands. ... This age is fraught with limitless perils, as well as untold possibilities" (in Conference Report, Oct. 1966, 4).

Please now listen to the voice of President Spencer W. Kimball, recorded in 1974, as he described the future of missionary work:

"I believe that the Lord is anxious to put into our hands inventions of which we laymen have hardly had a glimpse. ...

"With the Lord providing these miracles of communication, and with the increased efforts and devotion of our missionaries and all of us, and all others who are 'sent,' surely the divine injunction will come to pass: 'For, verily, the sound must go forth from this place into all the world, and unto the uttermost parts of the earth—the gospel must be preached unto every creature' (D&C 58:64)" ("When the World Will Be Converted," *Ensign,* Oct. 1974, 10–11).

And in 1981 President Gordon B. Hinckley taught: "We are confident that as the work of the Lord expands, he will inspire men to develop the means whereby the membership of the Church, wherever they may be, can be counseled in an intimate and personal way by his chosen prophet. Communication is the sinew that binds the Church as one great family. Between those facilities which are now available and those which are on the horizon, we shall be able to converse one with another according to the needs and circumstances of the time" ("Faith: The Essence of True Religion," *Ensign,* Nov. 1981, 5).

Messages and pictures that used to require days, weeks, and months to send and receive now can be communicated around the world in seconds. We thank thee, O God, for the prophets who have taught and prepared us for the time in which we live—and who have urged us to use technological advancements to support the ongoing mission of The Church of Jesus Christ of Latter-day Saints.

In June of 2013, Elder L. Tom Perry described the impact of digital technologies on missionary work. He said:

"When I was a young missionary, we were able to speak with contacts on the street and knock on doors to share the gospel. The world has changed since that time. Now, many people are involved in the busyness of their lives. They hurry here and there, and they are often less willing to allow complete strangers to enter their homes, uninvited, to share a message of the restored gospel. Their main point of contact with others, even with close friends, is often via the Internet. The very nature of missionary work, therefore, must change if the Lord is to accomplish His work of gathering Israel 'from the four corners of the earth' (2 Nephi 21:12). The missionaries are now authorized to use the Internet in their proselyting efforts. ...

"As missionaries enter this new age where they will use computers in the work of the Lord, we invite the young and the old, the adults, the young adults, the youth, and the children everywhere to join with us in this exciting new work by becoming Facebook friends with the missionaries in your area on your own computers and sharing their gospel messages online and by becoming involved in missionary work yourselves" ("Missionary Work in the Digital Age" [worldwide leadership training meeting, June 2013]; lds.org/broadcasts).

Approximately 40 percent of our worldwide missionary force soon will be using digital devices as tools in the work of conversion, retention, and activation. I am confident all of us also recognize how technology has accelerated family history and temple work, our individual and family study of the restored gospel, and made it possible for us to learn about, see, and experience the world in remarkable ways.

SOCIAL MEDIA

A technology known as social media is evolving in our day and playing an increasingly important role in hastening the work of salvation. The term *social media* refers to various channels of Internet and mobile-based communication that are used by individuals, families, and large groups of people to create digital communities wherein they share information, ideas, personal messages, and other content such as pictures and videos.

The popularity and reach of current social media tools are staggering. For example, Facebook is a networking service used to share messages, images, links, and videos with family, friends, and followers—and has approximately 1.2 billion average monthly users.

YouTube is a platform through which videos can be distributed, viewed, rated, and shared—and has approximately one billion average monthly users.

Twitter is a means of sending and receiving short, quick text messages and images called tweets—and has approximately 250 million average monthly users.

Instagram allows the sharing of pictures and short videos—and has approximately 150 million average monthly users.

Pinterest is a virtual bulletin board used to collect and share content and images from around the web—and has approximately 70 million average monthly users.

Please note that I have identified only five of the presently popular social media channels; many other such channels are being used by tens of millions of people. And new methods of and channels for digital communication are being developed constantly.

The Lord is hastening His work, and it is no coincidence that these powerful communication innovations and inventions are occurring in the dispensation of the fulness of times. Social media channels are global tools that can personally and positively impact large numbers of individuals and families. And I believe the time has come for us as disciples of Christ to use these inspired tools appropriately and more effectively to testify of God the Eternal Father, His plan of happiness for His children, and His Son, Jesus Christ, as the Savior of the world; to proclaim the reality of the Restoration of the gospel in the latter days; and to accomplish the Lord's work.

I now want to present several examples of gospel messages and images that have been created by the Church and by its members and communicated to the world through social media.

Example 1. Because of Him

To honor the true meaning of Easter, the Church earlier this year produced and distributed a two minute and 40 second video entitled *Because of Him*. This message focused on the hope, healing, and salvation made possible through the Atonement of Jesus Christ.

Because the Church, its members, and those of other faiths actively shared the video on social channels, it was viewed more than five million times during Easter week in 191 countries and territories of the world.

The Church also invited members and others to create and share their own Easter messages by using the #BecauseofHim hashtag. A hashtag is used to identify related social media messages. As a consequence of this initiative, numerous thoughts and images about the Savior and His Resurrection were communicated in many social channels and places, including Facebook, Twitter, and Instagram.

Example 2. Did You Think to Pray

Members of the Church and others published photos of themselves on Instagram, Facebook, Twitter, and other social channels with signs that completed the phrase "I pray when ..."

More than 300 photos were published. In addition, thousands of people used the #DidYouThinktoPray hashtag to share thoughts about when and why they communicate with their Heavenly Father.

Through the simple action of writing a few meaningful words on a small sign and sharing it on social media—something any of us can do—those who participated in this initiative touched hundreds of thousands of lives for the better and led to more than 40,000 conversations about the need for prayer.

Example 3. Book of Mormon 365

The Book of Mormon 365 Instagram account is a prime example of a simple idea that has allowed members to foster spiritual growth through social media.

The idea is simple. The account creators—Ben and Chelsea Prince from Arizona—post a reading assignment from the Book of Mormon every day. The assignments are divided into 365 pieces—the perfect size to allow followers to read the full Book of Mormon in one year.

The results have been astounding. More than 45,000 people now follow this Instagram account, with many of them actively sharing their thoughts and impressions with one another as they read the Book of Mormon together.

Example 4. General Authority Social Media Accounts

This summer the Church established an official Instagram account. In late June and early July, images were shared of President Monson and President Eyring at the Gilbert Arizona cultural celebration, President

Monson and President Eyring at a temple dedication, and President Ucht-dorf meeting a young girl during a recent trip to Switzerland.

What is unique about these photos? The members of the First Presidency themselves specifically chose the photos to be posted. You also may have noticed that some of the Brethren now have their own Twitter accounts, including Elder Ballard, Elder Holland, and me. Additional members of the Twelve may be active on Twitter in the near future. All of the Brethren also have their own Facebook pages on which they communicate important gospel messages.

Social media are helping the leaders and members of the restored Church to fulfill the Lord's mandate to "go ye into *all* the world, and preach the gospel to every creature" (Mark 16:15; italics added).

Example 5. #LDSconf

Many of you noticed the #LDSconf hashtag that was displayed on the lower left corner of the screen during the October 2013 and April 2014 general conference broadcasts. What you may not know is that members have used this hashtag to promote general conference for years. The first use of the #LDSconf hashtag dates back to October 2008, when it was created by a faithful member looking for an opportunity to follow and share conference-related tweets—long before the Church started using it.

As you can see from these examples on the screen, thousands of members join together twice a year to participate in the #LDSconf hashtag conversation about the things they learn and feel as they receive counsel from living prophets and apostles. Through this channel, millions of people around the world are edified by general conference messages.

Example 6. Meet the Mormons

I have one final example of gospel content that can be shared through social media channels.

A few years ago, the First Presidency approved the production of a feature-length film to help those not of our faith better understand Latter-day Saints as a people. This new film, titled *Meet the Mormons,* originally was scheduled to be shown exclusively in the Legacy Theater in Salt Lake City and in visitors' centers around the world. However, with the growth of the social media technologies we have discussed today, we realized that worldwide distribution of the film was now possible through various digital channels. As Elder M. Russell Ballard explained: "In Shakespeare's time, he was limited generally to the Globe Theatre, but we now have a global theater. ... The doors to the world are literally opened wide" ("When Shall These Things Be?" [Brigham Young University devotional, Mar. 12, 1996], 6; speeches.byu.edu).

Meet the Mormons addresses common misperceptions about our beliefs and highlights the blessings that come from living the gospel of Jesus Christ. The film will be released after October general conference in several media and channels—first in select theaters in the United States and then, later, in visitors' centers and on television, Internet movie channels, and social media channels. ...

For more information on the film, you can visit meetthemormons. com. This movie is one additional way members can share their beliefs with family and friends in a simple and effective way.

SOCIAL MEDIA GUIDELINES

These six examples of Church- and member-generated content illustrate several basic guidelines that should be followed as we use social media to convey gospel messages.

Be Authentic and Consistent

First, we are disciples and our messages should be authentic. A person or product that is not authentic is false, fake, and fraudulent. Our messages should be truthful, honest, and accurate. We should not exaggerate, embellish, or pretend to be someone or something we are not. Our content should be trustworthy and constructive. And anonymity on the Internet is not a license to be inauthentic.

Authenticity is strengthened through consistency. The gospel messages you share will be accepted more readily if your Christlike example is evident in the ongoing pattern of your posts.

Sister Bonnie L. Oscarson is a strong example of the power of consistency in social media. When called to serve as the Young Women general president in April of 2013, her Pinterest followers doubled overnight. Sister Oscarson's previous pins provided ample evidence of her integrity, prompting one blogger to ask, "Would your Pinterest page pass the Bonnie Oscarson test? ... Who will people decide you are if all they know is what is on your social media page?" (www.latterdaysaintwoman.com/would_your_pinterest_page_pass_the_bonnie_oscarson_test).

Edify and Uplift

Second, we and our messages should seek to edify and uplift rather than to argue, debate, condemn, or belittle. As Paul counseled the Ephesians, "Let no corrupt communication proceed out of your mouth, but that which is good to the use of edifying, that it may minister grace unto the hearers" (Ephesians 4:29).

Brothers and sisters, share the gospel with genuine love and concern for others. Be courageous and bold but not overbearing in sustaining and defending our beliefs, and avoid contention. As disciples our purpose should be to use social media channels as a means of projecting the light and truth of the restored gospel of Jesus Christ into a world that increasingly is dark and confused.

Respect Intellectual Property

Third, we and our messages should respect the property of other people and organizations. This simply means that you should not create your own content using someone else's art, name, photos, music, video, or other content without permission. To assist you in creating uplifting gospel messages, we are pleased to announce that the content in the Media Library on LDS.org, unless otherwise indicated, has been cleared for use by members without seeking permission from the Church. Additional information about the use of Church media can be found at social.lds.org.

When you share messages online, make sure others understand that you are expressing your personal thoughts and feelings. Please do not use the Church logo or otherwise suggest that you are speaking for or on behalf of the Church.

Be Wise and Vigilant

Fourth, be wise and vigilant in protecting yourself and those you love. We should remember that the Internet never forgets. Anything you communicate through a social media channel indeed will live forever—even if the app or program may promise otherwise. Only say it or post it if you want the entire world to have access to your message or picture for all time.

Following these simple guidelines will enable members of the Church around the world to create and share gospel messages that will cause the light to "shine forth out of darkness" (Mormon 8:16).

AN APOSTOLIC INVITATION

In my message, "Things as They Really Are," that I referred to earlier, I described some of the positive and negative consequences of computer-mediated communication. I highlighted the truth that technology in and of itself is neither inherently good nor bad. Rather, the purposes accomplished with and through technology are the ultimate indicators of goodness or badness.

I emphasize again what President David O. McKay indicated many years ago about the scientific discoveries of our age: "Discoveries latent with such potent power, either for the blessing or the destruction of human beings, as to make man's responsibility in controlling them the most gigantic ever placed in human hands. ... This age is fraught with limitless perils, as well as untold possibilities."

In "Things as They Really Are," I raised a voice of warning about the perils:

"I raise an apostolic voice of warning about the potentially stifling, suffocating, suppressing, and constraining impact of some kinds of cyberspace interactions and experiences upon our souls. The concerns I raise are not new; they apply equally to other types of media, such as television, movies, and music. But in a cyber world, these challenges are more pervasive and intense. I plead with you to beware of the sense-dulling and spiritually destructive influence of cyberspace technologies that are used to produce high fidelity and that promote degrading and evil purposes" (*Ensign,* June 2010, 20).

That warning is even more valid today than it was five years ago. Too much time can be wasted, too many relationships can be harmed or destroyed, and precious patterns of righteousness can be disrupted when technology is used improperly. We should not allow even good applications of social media to overrule the better and best uses of our time, energy, and resources.

These perils indeed are real, but so too are the extraordinary opportunities. I now want to build upon my previous warning about potential perils by extending an important invitation about powerful possibilities.

The examples of gospel messages we have seen today that were created for and conveyed through social media channels are wholesome, good, and have influenced positively tens of thousands of people. They represent an excellent beginning—but only a beginning. Let me briefly describe what I believe needs to come next.

In the seventh chapter of the book of Moses in the Pearl of Great

Price, Enoch foresees the Restoration of the gospel in the latter days, the gathering of Israel, the Second Coming of the Savior, and the return of Zion. I now invite your undivided attention as we consider together elements of four verses from this chapter:

"And Enoch beheld the Son of Man ascend up unto the Father; and he called unto the Lord, saying: ... wherefore, I ask thee if thou wilt not come again on the earth.

"And the Lord said unto Enoch: As I live, even so will I come in the last days, in the days of wickedness and vengeance. ...

"And the day shall come that the earth shall rest, but before that day the heavens shall be darkened, and a veil of darkness shall cover the earth; and the heavens shall shake, and also the earth; and great tribulations shall be among the children of men, but my people will I preserve;

"And righteousness will I send down out of heaven; and truth will I send forth out of the earth, to bear testimony of mine Only Begotten; his resurrection from the dead; yea, and also the resurrection of all men; and righteousness and truth will I cause *to sweep the earth as with a flood*" (Moses 7:59–62; italics added).

My beloved brothers and sisters, what has been accomplished thus far in this dispensation communicating gospel messages through social media channels is a good beginning—but only a small trickle. I now extend to you the invitation to help transform the trickle into a flood. Beginning at this place on this day, I exhort you to sweep the earth with messages filled with righteousness and truth—messages that are authentic, edifying, and praiseworthy—and literally to sweep the earth as with a flood.

I pray we will not simply participate in a flash flood that rises swiftly and then recedes just as rapidly. I am not suggesting a one-time glitzy initiative from which we quickly move on to the next task on our lengthy list of gospel things to do. We need not become social media experts or fanatics. And we do not need to spend inordinate amounts of time creating and disseminating elaborate messages. As Elder M. Russell Ballard recently taught, digital technologies should be our servants and not our masters (see M. Russell Ballard, "Be Still, and Know That I Am God" [Church Educational System devotional, May 4, 2014]; broadcasts.lds.org).

According to our desires and circumstances, each of us can contribute consistently to the growing flood of truth and righteousness. We should press forward using the Lord's pattern of "line upon line, precept upon precept, here a little and there a little" (2 Nephi 28:30).

Imagine the impact we can have as hundreds of thousands and millions of members of the Lord's restored Church contribute in seemingly small ways to the rising floodwaters. May our many small, individual efforts produce a steady rainfall of righteousness and truth that gradually swells a multitude of streams and rivers—and ultimately becomes a flood that sweeps the earth. "Wherefore, be not weary in well-doing, for ye are laying the foundation of a great work. And out of small things proceedeth that which is great" (D&C 64:33).

PROMISED BLESSINGS AND TESTIMONY

We have been and are blessed in so many ways; and where much is given, much is required. As an Apostle of the Lord Jesus Christ, I invoke this blessing upon you: that you may come to understand more fully the spiritual significance and blessing of living in the dispensation of the fulness of times, that you may have eyes to see clearly both the possibilities and the pitfalls of the remarkable technologies that are available to us today, that you may increase in your capacity to use these inspired tools appropriately, and that you may receive inspiration and guidance about the role you should play in helping to sweep the earth as with a flood of truth and righteousness. As you press forward in this holy work, I promise you will be blessed in mortality in the individual, specific, and necessary ways that will prepare you for eternity. I so bless you.

I witness the Father and the Son live. The Savior stands at the head of His Church in these latter days. He is hastening His work, and no unhallowed hand can stop this work from progressing. Of these things I testify in the sacred name of the Lord Jesus Christ, amen.

Education

Online Literacy Is a Lesser Kind

MARK BAUERLEIN

Slow reading counterbalances Web skimming. When Jakob Nielsen, a Web researcher, tested 232 people for how they read pages on screens, a curious disposition emerged. Dubbed by The New York Times "the guru of Web page 'usability,'" Nielsen has gauged user habits and screen experiences for years, charting people's online navigations and aims, using eye-tracking tools to map how vision moves and rests. In this study, he found that people took in hundreds of pages "in a pattern that's very different from what you learned in school." It looks like a capital letter F. At the top, users read all the way across, but as they proceed their descent quickens and horizontal sight contracts, with a slowdown around the middle of the page. Near the bottom, eyes move almost vertically, the lower-right corner of the page largely ignored. It happens quickly, too. "F for fast," Nielsen wrote in a column. "That's how users read your precious content."

The F-pattern isn't the only odd feature of online reading that Nielsen has uncovered in studies conducted through the consulting business Nielsen Norman Group (Donald A. Norman is a cognitive scientist who came from Apple; Nielsen was at Sun Microsystems). A decade ago, he issued an "alert" entitled "How Users Read on the Web." It opened bluntly: "They don't."

In the eye-tracking test, only one in six subjects read Web pages linearly, sentence by sentence. The rest jumped around chasing keywords, bullet points, visuals, and color and typeface variations. In another experiment on how people read e-newsletters, informational e-mail messages, and news feeds, Nielsen exclaimed, "'Reading' is not even the right word." The subjects usually read only the first two words in headlines, and they ignored the introductory sections. They wanted the "nut" and nothing else. A 2003 Nielsen warning asserted that a PDF file strikes users as a "content blob," and they won't read it unless they print it out. A "book-

Bauerlein, Mark. "Online Literacy Is a Lesser Kind." *The Chronicle Review*. 19 Sept. 2008. Web. 12 Mar. 2011. © The Chronicle of Higher Education, Inc.

like" page on screen, it seems, turns them off and sends them away. Another Nielsen test found that teenagers skip through the Web even faster than adults do, but with a lower success rate for completing tasks online (55 percent compared to 66 percent). Nielsen writes: "Teens have a short attention span and want to be stimulated. That's also why they leave sites that are difficult to figure out." For them, the Web isn't a place for reading and study and knowledge. It spells the opposite. "Teenagers don't like to read a lot on the Web. They get enough of that at school."

Those and other trials by Nielsen amount to an important research project that helps explain one of the great disappointments of education in our time. I mean the huge investment schools have made in technology, and the meager returns such funds have earned. Ever since the Telecommunications Act of 1996, money has poured into public-school classrooms. At the same time, colleges have raced to out-technologize one another. But while enthusiasm swells, e-bills are passed, smart classrooms multiply, and students cheer—the results keep coming back negative. When the Texas Education Agency evaluated its Technology Immersion Pilot, a $14-million program to install wireless tools in middle schools, the conclusion was unequivocal: "There were no statistically significant effects of immersion in the first year on either reading or mathematics achievement." When University of Chicago economists evaluated California schools before and after federal technology subsidies (the E-Rate program) had granted 30 percent more schools in the state Internet access, they determined that "the additional investments in technology generated by E-Rate had no immediate impact on measured student outcomes." In March 2007, the National Center for Education Evaluation and Regional Assistance evaluated 16 award-winning education technologies and found that "test scores were not significantly higher in classrooms using selected reading and mathematics software products." Last spring a New York State school district decided to drop its laptop program after years of offering it. The school-board president announced why: "After seven years, there was literally no evidence it had any impact on student achievement—none."

Those conclusions apply to middle-school and high-school programs, not to higher education (which has yet to produce any similarly large-scale evaluations). Nevertheless, the results bear consideration by those pushing for more e-learning on campuses.

Backers, providers, and fans of new technology explain the disappointing measures as a matter of circumstance. Teachers didn't get enough training, they say, or schoolwide coordination was spotty, parents not sufficiently involved. Maybe so, to some extent, but Nielsen's studies indicate another source. Digitized classrooms don't come through for an off-campus reason, a factor largely overlooked by educators. When they add laptops to classes and equip kids with on-campus digital tools, they add something else, too: the reading habits kids have developed after thousands of hours with those same tools in leisure time.

To teachers and professors, a row of glistening new laptops in their classroom after a dozen years with nothing but chalk and blackboard, or a podium that has been transformed from a wooden stand into a multimedia console, can appear a stunning conversion. But to the average freshman walking through the door and finding a seat, it's nothing new. Our students have worked and played with computers for years. The Horatio Alger Association found that students in high school use the Internet four and a half hours per week for help with homework (*The State of Our Nation's Youth*, 2008-2009), while the National School Boards Association measures social networking at nine hours per week, much of it spent on homework help. The gap between viewpoints is huge. Educators envision a whole new pedagogy with the tools, but students see only the chance to extend long-established postures toward the screen. If digitized classrooms did pose strong, novel intellectual challenges to students, we should see some pushback on their part, but few of them complain about having to learn in new ways.

Once again, this is not so much about the content students prefer—Facebook, YouTube, etc.—or whether they use the Web for homework or not. It is about the reading styles they employ. They race across the surface, dicing language and ideas into bullets and graphics, seeking what they already want and shunning the rest. They convert history, philosophy, literature, civics, and fine art into information, material to retrieve and pass along.

That's the drift of screen reading. Yes, it's a kind of literacy, but it breaks down in the face of a dense argument, a Modernist poem, a long political tract, and other texts that require steady focus and linear attention—in a word, slow reading. Fast scanning doesn't foster flexible minds that can adapt to all kinds of texts, and it doesn't translate into academic reading. If it did, then in a 2006 Chronicle survey of college professors, fully 41 percent wouldn't have labeled students "not well prepared" in reading (48 percent rated them "somewhat well prepared"). We would not find that the percentage of college graduates who reached "proficiency" literacy in 1992 was 40 percent, while in 2003 only 31 percent scored "proficient." We would see reading scores inching upward, instead of seeing, for instance, that the percentage of high-school students who reached proficiency dropped from 40 percent to 35 percent from 1992 to 2005.

And we wouldn't see even the better students struggling with "slow reading" tasks. In an "Introduction to Poetry" class awhile back, when I asked students to memorize 20 lines of verse and recite them to the others at the next meeting, a voice blurted, "Why?" The student wasn't being impudent or sullen. She just didn't see any purpose or value in the task. Canny and quick, she judged the plodding process of recording others' words a primitive exercise. Besides, if you can call up the verse any time with a click, why remember it? Last year when I required students in a literature survey course to obtain obituaries of famous writers without using the Internet, they stared in confusion. Checking a reference book, asking a librarian, and finding a microfiche didn't occur to them. So many free deliveries through the screen had sapped that initiative.

This is to say that advocates of e-learning in higher education pursue a risky policy, striving to unite liberal-arts learning with the very devices of acceleration that hinder it. Professors think they can help students adjust to using tools in a more sophisticated way than scattershot e-reading, but it's a lopsided battle. To repeat, college students have spent thousands of hours online acquiring faster and faster eyes and fingers before they even enter college, and they like the pace. It is unrealistic to expect 19-year-olds to perch before a screen and brake the headlong flight, even if it is the Declaration of Independence in hypertext coming through, not a buddy's message.

Some educators spot the momentum and shrug their shoulders, elevating screen scanning to equal status with slow reading. A notable instance occurred last year, when in an essay in The New York Times, Leah Price, a professor of English at Harvard University, criticized a report from the National Endowment for the Arts—"To Read or Not to Read" (to which I contributed)—precisely for downgrading digital scanning. Her article contained some errors of fact, such as that the 2004 NEA report "Reading at Risk" excluded nonfiction, but correctly singled out the NEA distinction between screen reading and print reading. To Price, it's a false one: "Bafflingly, the NEA's time-use charts classify 'e-mailing' and 'surfing Web sites' as competitors to reading, not subsets of it." Indeed, she said, to do so smacks of guile: "It takes some gerrymandering to make a generation logging ever more years in school, and ever more hours on the BlackBerry, look like nonreaders." (In truth, high-school students do no more in-class reading today than they did 20 years ago, according to a 2004 Department of Education report.)

What we are seeing is a strange flattening of the act of reading. It equates handheld screens with Madame Bovary, as if they made the same cognitive demands and inculcated the same habits of attention. It casts peeking at a text message and plowing through Middlemarch as subsets of one general activity. And it treats those quick bursts of words and icons as fully sufficient to sustain the reading culture. The long book may go, Price concluded, but reading will carry on just as it did before: "The file, the list, the label, the memo: These are the genres that will keep reading alive."

The step not taken here is a crucial one, namely to determine the relative effects of reading different "genres." We need an approach that doesn't let teachers and professors so cavalierly violate their charge as stewards of literacy. We must recognize that screen scanning is but one kind of reading, a lesser one, and that it conspires against certain intellectual habits requisite to liberal-arts learning. The inclination to read a huge Victorian novel, the capacity to untangle a metaphor in a line of verse, the desire to study and emulate a distant historical figure, the urge to ponder a concept such as Heidegger's ontic-ontological difference over and over and around and around until it breaks through as a transformative insight—those dispositions melt away with every 100 hours of browsing, blogging, IMing, Twittering, and Facebooking. The shape and tempo of online texts differ so much from academic texts that e-learning initiatives in college classrooms can't bridge them. Screen reading is a mind-set, and we should accept its variance from academic thinking. Nielsen concisely outlines the difference: "I continue to believe in the linear, author-driven narrative for educational purposes. I just don't believe the Web is optimal for delivering this experience. Instead, let's praise old narrative forms like books and sitting around a flickering campfire—or its modern-day counterpart, the PowerPoint projector," he says. "We should accept that the Web is too fast-paced for big-picture learning. No problem; we have other media, and each has its strengths. At the same time, the Web is perfect for narrow, just-in-time learning of information nuggets—so long as the learner already has the conceptual framework in place to make sense of the facts."

So let's restrain the digitizing of all liberal-arts classrooms. More than that, given the tidal wave of technology in young people's lives, let's frame a number of classrooms and courses as slow-reading (and slow-writing) spaces. Digital technology has become an imperial force, and it should meet more antagonists. Educators must keep a portion of the undergraduate experience disconnected, unplugged, and logged off. Pencils, blackboards, and books are no longer the primary instruments of learning, true, but they still play a critical role in the formation of intelligence, as countermeasures to information-age mores. That is a new mission for educators parallel to the mad rush to digitize learning, one that may seem reactionary and retrograde, but in fact strives to keep students' minds open and literacy broad. Students need to decelerate, and they can't do it by themselves, especially if every inch of the campus is on the grid.

Dear Students: Don't Let College Unplug Your Future

GIDEON BURTON

Dear students:

I'm about to say something a college professor shouldn't say to his students, but I care about you a lot so I'm prepared to break the code and say what needs to be said: *Your college experience is likely to set back your education, your career, and your creative potential.* Ironically, this will be done in the name of education. You deserve to know about this! You have what it takes to reclaim, reform, and remix your education. Don't let college unplug your future!

REALITY CHECK #1:
THE DIGITAL WORLD IS YOUR HOME CAMPUS

You already know this on some level. The campus for your education isn't made principally of buildings and books; it's made mostly of microchips and media. Any other "school" is a satellite now, subordinate to the main, digital campus where you reside and thrive. And since you grew up digital, you've been matriculated since the first click of a mouse button, with no need ever to graduate. Your world of learning and your world of play are seamless in the digital domain, and you are pretty much a senior on that campus, even in your teens. You spend your spare cash to get that iPhone or laptop, and you move effortlessly between virtual and physical worlds. The reality check is that physical schools and structured curricula and degree-seeking programs form a system that makes enormous demands upon you but which is fundamentally out of sync with the fact that your identity, development, education, and success will be intimately intertwined with the digital domain.

And why shouldn't they be? No generation of youth has ever lived in a more exciting era than ours nor learned in more compelling ways than are granted to you electronically today. Frontiers of opportunity have been opened for you through digital means that would make Cortés weep at how comparatively little spoil he carted off from the Aztecs. Each of you can reach across the planet, exploring the topography of our world with the ease of a soaring bird. You can befriend others from foreign places and cultures with the click of a key. You can get up to the minute updates from a robot on Mars on your cell phone, or Google Alexandrian libraries with an ease that would surpass the fantasies of generations of scholars. You can be a spectator to the cosmos or to the local city council meeting. But your new world does not leave you watching on the sidelines! You can share your lifestream, add your perspective to countless conversations, and have the world comment back—interacting with people who will value your ideas and your style. And what style! Modes of creative expression are being opened to your generation that none have known before. You can shape and share your identity in a thousand different ways, testing what you like, feeding your own passions, carving your own way. What a fantastic time to be alive!

REALITY CHECK #2: SURVIVING IN THE REAL WORLD

Hold on. It's one thing to trick out your avatar for the metaverse of your choice or suction Limewire for some fresh tracks, but what about earning your bread? Generations of parents and high school counselors have convinced you COLLEGE IS THE ANSWER. After all, how are you going to get a job if you can't show that shiny sheepskin to the suit across the desk from you in the personnel department? Blogging won't pay the bills! Maybe not.

REALITY CHECK #3: SHEEPSKIN VS. ONLINE IDENTITY

It will be a long time before a college diploma is as quaint as, say, getting a public notary's stamp. But there is another system already competing with college, and it will start those bean counters in the tuition office sweating soon enough. This alternative to college credentials is as huge as the Stay Puft marshmallow man from Ghostbusters and he's towering over the skyline right where town meets gown: online identity.

That's right. Who you are and what you've done will in the very near future be so well documented by your online activities that a résumé will be redundant. The time will come when a college degree will be suspect if not complemented by an admirable online record—and I'm not talking about transcripts. Your "transcripts" will consist of your lifestream: your blog, your social networks, your creative work published or otherwise represented online. Cyberspace is already more real to you than the physical space of your college campus—it is becoming so for your future employers.

Here's an old joke. Two farmers were strolling down the road. "Say, Joe, there's the new feller's mailbox. Whadya think them letters after his name stand fer?" "Well," says Joe, spitting some tobacco juice to one side, "everybody knows what BS stands for. MS must be 'more of the same.' But PhD? Couldn't tell you." His friend answers, "I know! 'Piled High and Deep!'"

Kinda lame, but it makes my point. Let me translate this into a real-life case. Recently at a nearby university there was a minor scandal because some big shot CEO was claiming he had a degree from the school, but in fact he did not. When the university reported this fact, do you know what the response from his company was? "Quit wasting our time. It's what he can do that matters, not where he graduated, and he does well for our company. Let's get back to work."

What people in my department always tell those seeking creative writing degrees will soon apply to every college major and student. "Look, if being in a degree program can give you a structure that will help you produce, it might be worth it. But in the end no one's going to care whether you have a degree or where it's from. Your work will speak for itself."

Speaking for yourself is what the new media is all about. And you don't have to raise your hand to be allowed to speak. You dont evin haf to spel rite, though that doesn't hurt. The credentialing system of college will ultimately prove less important than whether you use your college years to generate a body of visible and durable online work, openly accessible to the world, shouting who you are louder than any "graduated with honors" certification on a transcript one must pay to see.

Think about that the next time that you pull an all nighter for a term paper that will get thrown in the trash within the month. What you do online will last and will accumulate; much of what you do in college will disappear—unless, of course, you do for yourself what college will try to keep you from focusing on. You must consciously and conscientiously build your online presence. That's right. Invest in your future by one-upping the sheepskin before it disappears from significance like a lost mortar board thrown skyward at graduation ceremonies. If you are not visible online now, your diploma will be invisible later.

REALITY CHECK #4: THEY'RE GONNA SCARE YOU

Visible online! Are you crazy?! Plagiarism! Stalkers! Identity thieves! Old, vengeful girlfriends armed with Photoshop and your mother's maiden name! All those privacy issues! Even when it's safe it's a waste of time! *You should be more careful, my young friend, one's reputation is a very hard thing to rebuild, and you never know what harm you will bring on yourself...* Yada yada yada.

For good measure they will tell you stories like this one. "Haven't you heard about Mr. Online Idiot who got turned down for a job because the HR person Googled that unsavory picture from one of his less circumspect moments?"

Good point. Well, here's the flip side of that scenario. When I was evaluating applications for the presidency of a student club, the woman who got the job was the one that simply sent me to her blog, Spherical Chickens. What the hey? Spherical what? Past the catchy title I discovered a student with real thinking in her writing. Her blog showed the people with whom she connected and how invested she was in her schooling, her peers, and the literary life our club was all about. I recognized very quickly what she was capable of and qualified for. You see, she had been establishing herself for some time. Her online presence—all that thinking and linking and connecting. That was her résumé! You bet she got the job. She offered me her résumé, too, but she'd given me everything I needed to know with a single URL.

You need your own spherical chickens. Do you get it? A diploma is deadness, a sort of gravestone marking your time. A nice memorial, hopefully, but it isn't a living thing. But blogs are alive. They show your thinking and developing and working. Have you started one yet? Maybe tried out microblogging through Twitter or identi.ca? How about social bookmarking through Diigo or Delicious? Show me your think, students! And show the world, too. Show us how and where you connect, how you mash up your world. Be a DJ to your own groove. The tools are all there, and either free or cheap. People will be watching. People that count beyond your friend list on facebook. They already are watching, wondering why you aren't on the radar yet. Representing yourself well begins with showing up and revising on the fly. The ones waiting to get it perfect are on the sidelines of a game everyone gets to quarterback in. Why wait?

You'll wait because college is structured that way, dang it. Your college has a placement service, internships, an alumni network (hopefully). They have a structure that is going to help you succeed in life, right? Only far too many students reach the end of their four years of college like deer caught in headlights. It's only at that late date (or maybe in their senior year as they cross their fingers to get one of a few special internships...) that students start thinking they can present themselves to the world. ROFL!

Get online and get on the map! To be clear, lurkers aren't on the map. Googlers are online but search is unilateral. Email is online but sooooo 20th century, hiding the exchange of thought in the dark fiber of the net. No, the true Internet (what's been dubbed Web2.0) is an interactive grid, powered by the dynamic interplay of you talking and the web talking back and all of us involving/evolving one another's thoughts and creations. That's where you need to be online. Don't be your grandma glowing at being able to send a digital snap to you by email—unless your grandma also has a podcast or at least an RSS feed and is syndicating herself.

Is the Internet a time waste? Oh, yeah! Aren't there predators and scam artists and pornographers by the bitload? Yes. And shouldn't we all be careful not to get sucked into a black hole of any type? We should. But the biggest danger of the Internet in your generation is that people are keeping themselves from taking advantage of it. And I don't mean skimming some profits on eBay! I mean profiting from the social-intellectual matrix online. I know you get it, but do you get it all the way? Why are you holding yourself back? Students, you digital natives shouldn't put on the thinking cap of those digital immigrants who think the Internet is mostly a DANGER ZONE or that it has reached it's paramount utility by emailing a PDF of a scholarly article. Paleo-pathetic!

And here comes the triple whammy for college students. Once you are in the machine, clutching the sacred syllabus in one hand and shelling out Benjamins for textbooks with the other—once they have you on that semester cycle of credit hours and midterms and pressure deadlines that keep Rock Star and Prozac both in business—you simply can't squeeze in time for extras. <image of stressed coed> *If I don't finish that paper I will fail that class; if I fail that class I will not get that job. And besides, I have to be responsible!* <image of coed's mother in her head>

Holy trapped in Old School! Be responsible? For what? How about being responsible for your own future and your own education? Such irony here! We professors are instructed not to be the "sage on the stage" but to be the "guide on the side." We're told that students do better when they take initiative, teach themselves and one another. And they are right. And they do not even conceive of the fact that such self-directed learning is both available and should be happening beyond the artificial boundaries of classroom, semester, and campus. It's all good, all very progressive, provided you color inside the lines. Well, that's a photo filtered in sepia tone. Don't buy the rhetoric about inviting students to play a greater role in their education if that education is the walled garden of the status quo. That's not good enough for you. And don't buy the rhetoric that your university is blazing a trail with high tech when an old school paradigm prevails. <image of university magazine with supercomputer and smily nerd>

REALITY CHECK #5:
WHEN COLLEGE GETS TO 2.0, THEY'LL BE LATE FOR 3.0

My first title here was "castrating student opportunity by transforming college at the speed of lava," but I thought that was a bit strong, so I revised. My point is simply this: college is slow while learning is fast. Tooooo slow. Academia is an institution, and institutions by nature are conservative. They are built to resist change, even if they think they are accommodating it. There are reasons for such conservativeness—strong enough to be worth defending, but not at the mounting cost accumulating like Viagra spam in your junk mail filter. Behold! The INSANITY of the GLACIAL PACE of the OLD SCHOOL trying lamely to hipify itself:

"Hey, Phil. You're the department chair. We really need to be more current with what's going on with social media. I saw Michael Wesch's amazing Web2.0 video on YouTube and it was really inspiring."

"YouTube? I though the porn filters blocked that site."

"Yeah, well, I applied for an override code and finally got one last week. But anyway, we need to be studying blogs and wikis and such. Looks important."

"You're right, Candace. We've got to act on this immediately. Tell you what. Next Fall when the curriculum committee meets again, get them a proposal. Maybe they can approve a new course that will be ready for a faculty vote by December."

"Would I be able to teach the course on new media in January?"

"Well, it would still need to go up for college approval, then to the university. But I will definitely fast track it on my end. After all, this is timely stuff."

"So...maybe the following Fall?"

"Well, we have to have course catalog proposed changes in by October, but the curriculum committee won't meet until then. So it would be another full academic year before it was officially on the books, even with quick approvals. And you know Marty in the college..."

"The thing is, Phil, these students are really excited about all this. I was hoping to channel that excitement into some of their self-directed learning."

"It will only be a better class once it gets all that careful review. Besides, Candace, it will work in your favor. Let others work out the kinks with all that new technology so you don't have to."

"Hmmm. Well, in the meantime I suppose I could at least blog about some of these things."

"You're blogging? I thought you were finishing up that manuscript for University of Toronto Press. Look, I don't want to micromange your time, but tenure review is coming up. You might want to save some of those extras for after the important work is on the shelf."

"But the students are all blogging or talking about my courses already on Facebook. Some of them have even sent me friend requests. Maybe I should strike while the iron's hot."

"The Internet isn't going away, Candace. Just keep your eye on the ball for now. I know you want to help your students, but you don't serve them well if you don't get your scholarship done."

"Actually, I was thinking of trying to blog to them about my research. One of my students had an idea I thought would help the book along."

"Your students aren't your peers, Candace! You can tell them all about your research once it's finalized. Then it will trickle down into your teaching naturally."

"What about the provost telling us our students should come first?"

"He has tenure, Candace. That's when you can say those sorts of things."

So very chilling, but that's academia for you. Got a burning question? Let's put that on self-reflective ice until it's good and dead. How many Facebook updates had Candace's students posted just during the time of that conversation? Which of her students might have had a more meaningful experience if his education and her research were a two-way conversation that he and she both dared themselves to engage in?

But that's not what all that computer infrastructure is for in college. It's not there to bring the pursuit of knowledge (teaching) onto the same plane as The Pursuit of Knowledge (big people research). No, your college wants to dazzle you with spiffy computer labs and brag it up that the Internet is piped into the dorm rooms, but the whole structure of college works against the best educational uses of the web no matter how wired the buildings are. So much oversight and review has been worked into the hierarchy and politics of higher education that it has made itself incapable of valuing or accommodating the very media and methods that could accelerate your learning. It ain't right, and there it is.

College is trapped inside of its ways, and it wants to keep you there and make you believe that ONLY THROUGH THE GRACE OF ITS CURRICULUM AND DEGREES AND SUPER SPECIAL EXPERTS AND ACCESS TO ITS PRECIOUS STORE OF SUB-SCRIPTION-ONLY SCHOLARSHIP WILL YOU EVER DO OR SAY ANYTHING OF VALUE. Moreover, "We're going to put a hold on your graduation until that library book is returned!" Me SKARED!!

Hey! Don't believe what the system preaches by its structure! You can graduate to engaging with the world right now!

Here's another scenario to illustrate how college can't help itself from retarding educational progress because of its very structure. Let's say a professor comes back from a conference jazzed about using blogs and wikis. His college is with it enough to say, "You bet! Blog away! We'll alert the alumni magazine editor!" *But hold on just a bit. You know, we have an IT team looking into what the best blogging system is and how to handle the back end of data demand, and of course the Blackboard course management system that the university spent half its endowment on has been promising blogging in its next module and we'll need to get that up and going with a pilot group to work the kinks out for a semester or two. And wikis? Well, we can't have students having direct access changing data on university servers. We don't have the firewalls or oversight needed for that can of worms, and it will take some time to evaluate which third-party blogging or wiki platforms could be an alternative...*

And that is how Web2.0 dies in college when college administrators think they are bringing it to life. Kinda puts the iron in ironic. Ouch!

But they deserve our pity, really. They just can't help themselves. They, too, are victims of the system. They can't help but kill the things that would bring your education to life. Oh, the humanities!

REALITY CHECK #6: SCHOOL IMPEDES EDUCATION

Listen to me, students! Your education is far too important to wait for academia to catch up! The train is moving, and you know it! You're already on it! You are connecting to each other through peer2peer, social networks, and text messaging. Don't even get me started on video games! Get a Second Life! But the old guard just makes you feel guilty about it, as though every text message were a drug deal you were recklessly thumbing while driving a carload of toddlers without seat belts. No, we profs make you check your tech at the door, keeping sacred our little patch of control—all while, VOLUNTARILY, the whole tribe of today's youth has adopted and worked into their daily lives the greatest educational delivery system of the century—the cell phone. Your personal tech needs to be taken more seriously, students, not treated as an impediment to learning! Turn your cell phone off in the theater, but not in the theater of learning! yuk yuk

I give my students my cell phone number so they can text or twitter me right from mid-think, and you know what? It's great to be part of this dynamic system of learning that these new technologies enable. Are you going to trust your education to those scaredy-profs that won't let you in on what they are doing in their closed-science lab or won't deal with you except when you are in class or during office hours?

So here's the thing. You can't change them. The system will just roll you if you try. The answer? Don't burn down the campus. No, just treat your classes like you do your CDs—rip, trade, and burn the best tracks, deleting what doesn't fit your playlist. YOU are going to be the change, the generation that replaces those too blinded by the pride of custom to recognize that mighty fireball of knowledge and connection blazing through the bright fiber of our computers—only to be firewalled and fizzled by the man. You stand on the shoulders of pygmies.

If you are in college or headed that way, you are going to have to see its structure as the impediment that it will doggedly strive to be. And they are just gearing up for the real fight. You thought the music industry was playing dirty and showing their true, tawdry colors? Just watch and see how much colleges will push back, insisting on the precious nature of their way of receiving, transmitting, and approving knowledge. What a tantrum we are in for! <image: girl throwing tantrum> "Nuh-uh! WE say how to learn, where to learn, what to learn. WE SAY!!" They will proudly wave the flag of tradition and the brand of their school—as though their university were more than a portal on the world, as though their campus were in fact the world, as though education itself were a commodity they could brand, rather than a way of engaging the world. They will lose their credibility in being able to give meaningful shape to your future if they freeze your modes of learning in the past.

Don't let them shape you into a drone that believes he or she is not credentialed to think, speak, act, or create unless it is in terms of their syllabus, their "terms," their degrees. Unfortunately, colleges will (like the RIAA) prove themselves not to be about the "music" but all about the business. If colleges really believed what they preached about general education and preparing students for the world, their leaders would cut the Gordian knot of red tape and cover-one's-butt bureaucracy and usher in the new paradigm. They could help to accelerate the evolution of learning by opening up their concepts of what kind of knowledge is valuable, and they would value you students for real—not patronizingly but authentically—for what you can really do and be within that magnificent world that is your playground and privilege to explore, digest, remix, and rebuild. But it won't happen in college. The great and spacious building of academia is the pride of the world—an increasingly pinched and persnickety world of self-congratulating experts swallowed in the solipsism of their esoteric inspeak. Oh gads, I'm infected myself!

Academia still has power; college still matters, but you don't have to play the game. Don't check yourself when you have the urge to connect, explore, create, and express. Use the tools at hand. Feel the energy of living knowledge sustained by the new media. Don't sit in the voluntary detention of self-censorship, kept from more involved participation online by worries over whether you will get a good grade in college. Give yourself the best grades ever by claiming what is offered to you tuition-free. Find those crazed teachers (typically adjuncts and grad students with less to lose) who have not been lobotomized by the moribund methodology of conventional learning and teaching. Trust the ones who give you their cell phone numbers and who light up when you make a blog post tangentially related to that course but something you are passionate about. In that earlier cultural revolution, they said, "Don't trust anyone over 30." No, that's not it. The digitally sympathetic are a minority, but they are everywhere that you can find them, and that's more likely to be on Facebook than in the marble hallways of the Widener library at Hahvard.

Sincerely,

A concerned professor

Twitter me at wakingtiger :)

Teaching to the Text Message

ANDY SELSBERG

I'VE been teaching college freshmen to write the five-paragraph essay and its bully of a cousin, the research paper, for years. But these forms invite font-size manipulation, plagiarism and clichés. We need to set our sights not lower, but shorter.

I don't expect all my graduates to go on to Twitter-based careers, but learning how to write concisely, to express one key detail succinctly and eloquently, is an incredibly useful skill, and more in tune with most students' daily chatter, as well as the world's conversation. The photo caption has never been more vital.

So a few years ago, I started slipping my classes short writing assignments alongside the required papers. Once, I asked them, "Come up with two lines of copy to sell something you're wearing now on eBay." The mix of commerce and fashion stirred interest, and despite having 30 students in each class, I could give everyone serious individual attention. For another project, I asked them to describe the essence of the chalkboard in one or two sentences. One student wrote, "A chalkboard is a lot like memory: often jumbled, unorganized and sloppy. Even after it's erased, there are traces of everything that's been written on it."

This was great, but I want to go shorter. Like many who teach, I keep thinking the perfect syllabus is a semester away—with just a few tweaks, and maybe a total pedagogical overhaul. My ideal composition class would include assignments like "Write coherent and original comments for five YouTube videos, quickly telling us why surprised kittens or unconventional wedding dances resonate with millions," and "Write Amazon reviews, including a bit of summary, insight and analysis, for three canonical works we read this semester (points off for gratuitous modern argot and emoticons)."

The longest assignment could be a cover letter, and even that might be streamlined to a networking e-mail. I'd rather my students master skills like these than proper style for citations.

Selsberg, Andy. "Teaching to the Text Message." *The New York Times*. 19 Mar. 2011. Web. 21 Mar. 2011. © The New York Times Company.

A lot can be said with a little—the mundane and the extraordinary. Philosophers like Confucius ("Learning without thought is labor lost. Thought without learning is perilous.") and Nietzsche were kings of the aphorism.

And short isn't necessarily a shortcut. When you have only a sentence or two, there's nowhere to hide. I'm not suggesting that colleges eliminate long writing projects from English courses, but maybe we should save them for the second semester. Rewarding concision first will encourage students to be economical and innovative with language. Who knows, we might even start to leave behind text messages and comment threads that our civilization can be proud of.

How Computers Change the Way We Think

SHERRY TURKLE

The tools we use to think change the ways in which we think. The invention of written language brought about a radical shift in how we process, organize, store, and transmit representations of the world. Although writing remains our primary information technology, today when we think about the impact of technology on our habits of mind, we think primarily of the computer.

My first encounters with how computers change the way we think came soon after I joined the faculty at the Massachusetts Institute of Technology in the late 1970s, at the end of the era of the slide rule and the beginning of the era of the personal computer. At a lunch for new faculty members, several senior professors in engineering complained that the transition from slide rules to calculators had affected their students' ability to deal with issues of scale. When students used slide rules, they had to insert decimal points themselves. The professors insisted that that required students to maintain a mental sense of scale, whereas those who relied on calculators made frequent errors in orders of magnitude. Additionally, the students with calculators had lost their ability to do "back of the envelope" calculations, and with that, an intuitive feel for the material.

That same semester, I taught a course in the history of psychology. There, I experienced the impact of computational objects on students' ideas about their emotional lives. My class had read Freud's essay on slips of the tongue, with its famous first example: The chairman of a parliamentary session opens a meeting by declaring it closed. The students discussed how Freud interpreted such errors as revealing a person's mixed emotions. A computer-science major disagreed with Freud's approach. The mind, she argued, is a computer. And in a computational dictionary—like we have in the human mind—"closed" and "open" are designated by the same symbol, separated by a sign for opposition. "Closed" equals "minus open."

Turkle, Sherry. "How Computers Change the Way We Think." *Chronicle of Higher Education.* 30 Jan. 2004. Web. 14 Mar. 2011. © The Chronicle of Higher Education, Inc.

To substitute "closed" for "open" does not require the notion of ambivalence or conflict.

"When the chairman made that substitution," she declared, "a bit was dropped; a minus sign was lost. There was a power surge. No problem."

The young woman turned a Freudian slip into an information-processing error. An explanation in terms of meaning had become an explanation in terms of mechanism.

Such encounters turned me to the study of both the instrumental and the subjective sides of the nascent computer culture. As an ethnographer and psychologist, I began to study not only what the computer was doing *for* us, but what it was doing *to* us, including how it was changing the way we see ourselves, our sense of human identity.

In the 1980s, I surveyed the psychological effects of computational objects in everyday life—largely the unintended side effects of people's tendency to project thoughts and feelings onto their machines. In the 20 years since, computational objects have become more explicitly designed to have emotional and cognitive effects. And those "effects by design" will become even stronger in the decade to come. Machines are being designed to serve explicitly as companions, pets, and tutors. And they are introduced in school settings for the youngest children.

Today, starting in elementary school, students use e-mail, word processing, computer simulations, virtual communities, and PowerPoint software. In the process, they are absorbing more than the content of what appears on their screens. They are learning new ways to think about what it means to know and understand.

What follows is a short and certainly not comprehensive list of areas where I see information technology encouraging changes in thinking. There can be no simple way of cataloging whether any particular change is good or bad. That is contested terrain. At every step we have to ask, as educators and citizens, whether current technology is leading us in directions that serve our human purposes. Such questions are not technical; they are social, moral, and political. For me, addressing that subjective side of computation is one of the more significant challenges for the next decade of information technology in higher education. Technology does not determine change, but it encourages us to take certain directions. If we make those directions clear, we can more easily exert human choice.

THINKING ABOUT PRIVACY

Today's college students are habituated to a world of online blogging, instant messaging, and Web browsing that leaves electronic traces. Yet they have had little experience with the right to privacy. Unlike past generations of Americans, who grew up with the notion that the privacy of their mail was sacrosanct, our children are accustomed to electronic surveillance as part of their daily lives.

I have colleagues who feel that the increased incursions on privacy have put the topic more in the news, and that this is a positive change. But middle-school and high-school students tend to be willing to provide personal information online with no safeguards, and college students seem uninterested in violations of privacy and in increased governmental and commercial surveillance. Professors find that students do not understand that in a democracy, privacy is a right, not merely a privilege. In 10 years, ideas about the relationship of privacy and government will require even more active pedagogy. (One might also hope that increased education about the kinds of silent surveillance that technology makes possible may inspire more active political engagement with the issue.)

AVATARS OR A SELF?

Chat rooms, role-playing games, and other technological venues offer us many different contexts for presenting ourselves online. Those possibilities are particularly important for adolescents because they offer what Erik Erikson described as a moratorium, a time out or safe space for the personal experimentation that is so crucial for adolescent development. Our dangerous world—with crime, terrorism, drugs, and AIDS—offers little in the way of safe spaces. Online worlds can provide valuable spaces for identity play.

But some people who gain fluency in expressing multiple aspects of self may find it harder to develop authentic selves. Some children who write narratives for their screen avatars may grow up with too little experience of how to share their real feelings with other people. For those who are lonely yet afraid of intimacy, information technology has made it possible to have the illusion of companionship without the demands of friendship.

FROM POWERFUL IDEAS TO POWERPOINT

In the 1970s and early 1980s, some educators wanted to make programming part of the regular curriculum for K-12 education. They argued that because information technology carries ideas, it might as well carry the most powerful ideas that computer science has to offer. It is ironic that in most elementary schools today, the ideas being carried by information technology are not ideas from computer science like procedural thinking, but more likely to be those embedded in productivity tools like Power-Point presentation software.

PowerPoint does more than provide a way of transmitting content. It carries its own way of thinking, its own aesthetic—which not surprisingly shows up in the aesthetic of college freshmen. In that aesthetic, presentation becomes its own powerful idea.

To be sure, the software cannot be blamed for lower intellectual standards. Misuse of the former is as much a symptom as a cause of the latter. Indeed, the culture in which our children are raised is increasingly a culture of presentation, a corporate culture in which appearance is often more important than reality. In contemporary political discourse, the bar has also been lowered. Use of rhetorical devices at the expense of cogent argument regularly goes without notice. But it is precisely because standards of intellectual rigor outside the educational sphere have fallen that educators must attend to how we use, and when we introduce, software that has been designed to simplify the organization and processing of information.

In "The Cognitive Style of PowerPoint" (Graphics Press, 2003), Edward R. Tufte suggests that PowerPoint equates bulleting with clear thinking. It does not teach students to begin a discussion or construct a narrative. It encourages presentation, not conversation. Of course, in the hands of a master teacher, a PowerPoint presentation with few words and powerful images can serve as the jumping-off point for a brilliant lecture. But in the hands of elementary-school students, often introduced to PowerPoint in the third grade, and often infatuated with its swooshing sounds, animated icons, and flashing text, a slide show is more likely to close down debate than open it up.

Developed to serve the needs of the corporate boardroom, the software is designed to convey absolute authority. Teachers used to tell students that clear exposition depended on clear outlining, but presentation software has fetishized the outline at the expense of the content.

Narrative, the exposition of content, takes time. PowerPoint, like so much in the computer culture, speeds up the pace.

WORD PROCESSING VS. THINKING

The catalog for the Vermont Country Store advertises a manual type-writer, which the advertising copy says "moves at a pace that allows time to compose your thoughts." As many of us know, it is possible to manipulate text on a computer screen and see how it looks faster than we can think about what the words mean.

Word processing has its own complex psychology. From a pedagogical point of view, it can make dedicated students into better writers because it allows them to revise text, rearrange paragraphs, and experiment with the tone and shape of an essay. Few professional writers would part with their computers; some claim that they simply cannot think without their hands on the keyboard. Yet the ability to quickly fill the page, to see it before you can think it, can make bad writers even worse.

A seventh grader once told me that the typewriter she found in her mother's attic is "cool because you have to type each letter by itself. You have to know what you are doing in advance or it comes out a mess." The idea of thinking ahead has become exotic.

TAKING THINGS AT INTERFACE VALUE

We expect software to be easy to use, and we assume that we don't have to know how a computer works. In the early 1980s, most computer users who spoke of transparency meant that, as with any other machine, you could "open the hood" and poke around. But only a few years later, Macintosh users began to use the term when they talked about seeing their documents and programs represented by attractive and easy-to-interpret icons. They were referring to an ability to make things work without needing to go below the screen surface. Paradoxically, it was the screen's opacity that permitted that kind of transparency. Today, when people say that something is transparent, they mean that they can see how to make it work, not that they know how it works. In other words, transparency means epistemic opacity.

The people who built or bought the first generation of personal computers understood them down to the bits and bytes. The next generation of operating systems were more complex, but they still invited that old-time reductive understanding. Contemporary information technology encourages different habits of mind. Today's college students are already used to taking things at (inter) face value; their successors in 2014 will be even less accustomed to probing below the surface.

SIMULATION AND ITS DISCONTENTS

Some thinkers argue that the new opacity is empowering, enabling anyone to use the most sophisticated technological tools and to experiment with simulation in complex and creative ways. But it is also true that our tools carry the message that they are beyond our understanding. It is possible that in daily life, epistemic opacity can lead to passivity.

I first became aware of that possibility in the early 1990s, when the first generation of complex simulation games were introduced and immediately became popular for home as well as school use. SimLife teaches the principles of evolution by getting children involved in the development of complex ecosystems; in that sense it is an extraordinary learning tool. During one session in which I played SimLife with Tim, a 13-year-old, the screen before us flashed a message: "Your orgot is being eaten up." "What's an orgot?" I asked. Tim didn't know. "I just ignore that," he said confidently. "You don't need to know that kind of stuff to play."

For me, that story serves as a cautionary tale. Computer simulations enable their users to think about complex phenomena as dynamic, evolving systems. But they also accustom us to manipulating systems whose core assumptions we may not understand and that may not be true.

We live in a culture of simulation. Our games, our economic and political systems, and the ways architects design buildings, chemists envisage molecules, and surgeons perform operations all use simulation technology. In 10 years the degree to which simulations are embedded in every area of life will have increased exponentially. We need to develop a new form of media literacy: readership skills for the culture of simulation.

We come to written text with habits of readership based on centuries of civilization. At the very least, we have learned to begin with the journalist's traditional questions: who, what, when, where, why, and how. Who wrote these words, what is their message, why were they written, and how are they situated in time and place, politically and socially? A central project for higher education during the next 10 years should be creating programs in information-technology literacy, with the goal of teaching students to interrogate simulations in much the same spirit, challenging their built-in assumptions.

Despite the ever-increasing complexity of software, most computer environments put users in worlds based on constrained choices. In other words, immersion in programmed worlds puts us in reassuring environments where the rules are clear. For example, when you play a video game, you often go through a series of frightening situations that you escape by mastering the rules—you experience life as a reassuring dichotomy of scary and safe. Children grow up in a culture of video games, action films, fantasy epics, and computer programs that all rely on that familiar scenario of almost losing but then regaining total mastery: There is danger. It is mastered. A still-more-powerful monster appears. It is subdued. Scary. Safe.

Yet in the real world, we have never had a greater need to work our way out of binary assumptions. In the decade ahead, we need to rebuild the culture around information technology. In that new sociotechnical culture, assumptions about the nature of mastery would be less absolute. The new culture would make it easier, not more difficult, to consider life in shades of gray, to see moral dilemmas in terms other than a battle between Good and Evil. For never has our world been more complex, hybridized, and global. Never have we so needed to have many contradictory thoughts and feelings at the same time. Our tools must help us accomplish that, not fight against us.

Information technology is identity technology. Embedding it in a culture that supports democracy, freedom of expression, tolerance, diversity, and complexity of opinion is one of the next decade's greatest challenges. We cannot afford to fail.

When I first began studying the computer culture, a small breed of highly trained technologists thought of themselves as "computer people." That is no longer the case. If we take the computer as a carrier of a way of knowing, a way of seeing the world and our place in it, we are all computer people now.

Why the Smart Reading Device of the Future May Be ... Paper

BRANDON KEIM

Paper books were supposed to be dead by now. For years, information theorists, marketers, and early adopters have told us their demise was imminent. Ikea even redesigned a bookshelf to hold something other than books. Yet in a world of screen ubiquity, many people still prefer to do their serious reading on paper.

Count me among them. When I need to read deeply—when I want to lose myself in a story or an intellectual journey, when focus and comprehension are paramount—I still turn to paper. Something just feels fundamentally richer about reading on it. And researchers are starting to think there's something to this feeling.

To those who see dead tree editions as successors to scrolls and clay tablets in history's remainder bin, this might seem like literary Luddism. But I e-read often: when I need to copy text for research or don't want to carry a small library with me. There's something especially delicious about late-night sci-fi by the light of a Kindle Paperwhite.

What I've read on screen seems slippery, though. When I later recall it, the text is slightly translucent in my mind's eye. It's as if my brain better absorbs what's presented on paper. Pixels just don't seem to stick. And often I've found myself wondering, why might that be?

The usual explanation is that internet devices foster distraction, or that my late-thirty-something brain isn't that of a true digital native, accustomed to screens since infancy. But I have the same feeling when I am reading a screen that's not connected to the internet and Twitter or online Boggle can't get in the way. And research finds that kids these days consistently prefer their textbooks in print rather than pixels. Whatever the answer, it's not just about habit.

Another explanation, expressed in a recent *Washington Post* article on the decline of deep reading, blames a sweeping change in our lifestyles: We're all so multi-tasked and attention-fragmented that our brains are losing the ability to focus on long, linear texts. I certainly feel this way, but if I don't read deeply as often or easily as I used to, it does still happen. It just doesn't happen on screen, and not even on devices designed specifically for that experience.

Maybe it's time to start thinking of paper and screens another way: not as an old technology and its inevitable replacement, but as different and complementary interfaces, each stimulating particular modes of thinking. Maybe paper is a technology uniquely suited for imbibing novels and essays and complex narratives, just as screens are for browsing and scanning.

"Reading is human-technology interaction," says literacy professor Anne Mangen of Norway's University of Stavenger. "Perhaps the tactility and physical permanence of paper yields a different cognitive and emotional experience." This is especially true, she says, for "reading that can't be done in snippets, scanning here and there, but requires sustained attention."

*   *   *

Mangen is among a small group of researchers who study how people read on different media. It's a field that goes back several decades, but yields no easy conclusions. People tended to read slowly and somewhat inaccurately on early screens. The technology, particularly e-paper, has improved dramatically, to the point where speed and accuracy aren't now problems, but deeper issues of memory and comprehension are not yet well-characterized.

Complicating the scientific story further, there are many types of reading. Most experiments involve short passages read by students in an academic setting, and for this sort of reading, some studies have found no obvious differences between screens and paper. Those don't necessarily capture the dynamics of deep reading, though, and nobody's yet run the sort of experiment, involving thousands of readers in real-world conditions who are tracked for years on a battery of cognitive and psychological measures, that might fully illuminate the matter.

In the meantime, other research does suggest possible differences. A 2004 study found that students more fully remembered what they'd read on paper. Those results were echoed by an experiment that looked specifically at e-books, and another by psychologist Erik Wästlund at Sweden's

Karlstad University, who found that students learned better when reading from paper.

Wästlund followed up that study with one designed to investigate screen reading dynamics in more detail. He presented students with a variety of on-screen document formats. The most influential factor, he found, was whether they could see pages in their entirety. When they had to scroll, their performance suffered.

According to Wästlund, scrolling had two impacts, the most basic being distraction. Even the slight effort required to drag a mouse or swipe a finger requires a small but significant investment of attention, one that's higher than flipping a page. Text flowing up and down a page also disrupts a reader's visual attention, forcing eyes to search for a new starting point and re-focus.

'Those dead trees still have a lot of life in them. 'Scrolling "took a lot of mental resources that could have been spent comprehending the text instead," said Wästlund. Like being distracted when memorizing a phone number, scrolling's interruptions knocked information from short-term memory. That's the basic level of information processing, laying a foundation for long-term memories and knowledge.

To be sure, electronic reading has changed quite a bit since Wästlund's experiments, which concluded in 2005. Many applications, such as Amazon's Kindle software, have scrapped scrolling in favor of page-flipping emulations. Yet Mangen, who in a 2013 study of Norwegian teens found a deeper comprehension of texts on paper, and Wästlund say that e-readers may fail to capture a crucial, generally overlooked aspect of paper books: their physicality.

From this perspective, the feel of pages under one's fingertips isn't simply old-fashioned charm. It's a rich source of information, subconsciously informing readers of their position in a text. Reading experts say that sense of position is important: It provides a sort of conceptual scaffold on which information and memory is automatically arranged, and the scaffold is strongest when built from both visual and tactile cues.

"All those cues like what the page looks like, what the book felt like, all those little pieces help you put together the whole thing," said Marilyn Jager-Adams, a cognitive psychologist and literacy expert at Brown University. "And they are just impoverished on a Kindle or tablet"—though these devices can be improved.

Electronic interfaces do feature symbolic progress bars or percentage-remaining figures, but these are purely visual stimuli, rather than tactile. Pages also tend to be displayed individually rather than in pairs, further limiting spatial representation. And in a sense, e-readers and tablets really just consist of a single page that's constantly being re-written. That immateriality could register differently than fixed texts.

Paper books also allow for different types of annotation: underlining and dog-earing and margin-scribbling, which for many people is integral to deep reading. Screen-reading software may allow annotations, but the process is far less tactile—and some researchers say tactility may be important. Studies have shown that close links exist between gesture and cognition. These links are little-studied in the context of reading, but are very much a part of writing, which similarly involves constructing mental models of text.

"Especially for those of us with lots of traditional book exposure, we use physical pages as anchors for deep comprehension," said cognitive scientist Jenny Thomson of Sheffield University. Thomson describes reading comprehension as having several levels: individual words and sentences, which should be equivalent on screen and paper, and ultimately the larger narrative structure they build.

Keeping that structure in mind allows for richer comprehension, weaving themes and threads of thoughts into insight, and for some people, this may be easier with paper. "E-paper takes away this comprehension prop to some degree," Thomson said, "which I think could have subtle impacts for many people, at least until their reading system learns to adapt."

Jager-Adams agrees: "I think until they solve those problems, there are a number of people who will find that reading longer, more complex texts is difficult on a Kindle or tablet."

* * *

Other research points to additional differences. Rakefet Ackerman at the Technion-Israel Institute of Technology has found that students reading on paper and screen may think differently about their own learning processes.

When reading on paper, Ackerman's students seemed to have a better sense of their own understanding. When reading on screen, they thought they absorbed information readily, but tests showed otherwise. Screens seemed to foster overconfidence. With practice, this could be corrected, said Ackerman, but "the natural learning process on paper is more thorough than on screen."

Ackerman also noted, however, that preference played an important role. When students preferred screen reading, they learned less when required to read from paper, and vice versa.

Much of this research jibes with my own experience, but the science is far from settled. A study by psychologist Sara Margolin of Brockport University found no difference in reading comprehension in students reading paper, computer screens and e-readers. "It's really a matter of personal preference," said Margolin.

Another study of students using paper and electronic textbooks found no significant differences—and for some readers, such as those with dyslexia who find it easier to concentrate on small sections of text, Thomson found that e-readers may already be superior to paper books. "I think as we have more and more ways to present digital text, we will see more of these 'interactions' where for one group of readers, we see an advantage, and for others we see the opposite," said Thomson.

Many questions remain. If reading shorter texts on screen or paper is indeed a matter of preference, does the same hold for deep reading? Can interface designers find better workarounds for the physical limitations of screens? Will people eventually adapt, with screen-trained readers finding new ways of creating structures in the absence of tactile cues?

Jager-Adams thinks it's possible that deep reading, at least for many people, may eventually prove to be intertwined with the physical form of paper books. If that's true, it's all the more reason to appreciate them.

"We should be wary of saying, 'That's the way we're going to read in the future anyways, so why resist?'" said Mangen. "There is something to deep reading and deep thinking that is worth making an effort to preserve." Whether we need paper to do that remains to be seen. For now, though, there's still plenty of life in those dead trees.

The Real Revolution in Online Education Isn't MOOCs

MICHELLE WEISE

Data is confirming what we already know: recruiting is an imprecise activity, and degrees don't communicate much about a candidate's potential and fit. Employers need to know what a student knows and can do.

Something is clearly wrong when only 11% of business leaders—compared to 96% of chief academic officers—believe that graduates have the requisite skills for the workforce. It's therefore unlikely that business leaders are following closely what's going on in higher education. Even the latest hoopla around massive open online courses (MOOCs) amounts to more of the same: academics designing courses that correspond with their own interests rather than the needs of the workforce, but now doing it online.

But there is a new wave of online competency-based learning providers that has absolutely nothing to do with offering free, massive, or open courses. In fact, they're not even building courses per se, but creating a whole new architecture of learning that has serious implications for businesses and organizations around the world.

It's called online competency-based education, and it's going to revolutionize the workforce.

Say a newly minted graduate with a degree in history realizes that in order to attain her dream job at Facebook, she needs some experience with social media marketing. Going back to school is not a desirable option, and many schools don't even offer relevant courses in social

Michelle R. Weise, Ph.D. is a senior research fellow in higher education at the Clayton Christensen Institute for Disruptive Innovation and co-author with Clayton M. Christensen of Hire Education: Mastery, Modularization, and the Workforce Revolution.

Weise, Michelle. "The Real Revolution in Online Education Isn't MOOCs." *Harvard Business Review.* Harvard Business Publishing, 17 Oct. 2014. Web. <http://blogs.hbr.org/2014/10/the-real-revolution-in-online-education-isnt-moocs/>. © Harvard Business School Publishing.

media. Where is the affordable, accessible, targeted, and high-quality program that she needs to skill-up?

Online competency-based education is the key to filling in the skills gaps in the workforce. Broadly speaking, competency-based education identifies explicit learning outcomes when it comes to knowledge and the application of that knowledge. They include measurable learning objectives that empower students: this person can apply financial principles to solve business problems; this person can write memos by evaluating seemingly unrelated pieces of information; or this person can create and explain big data results using data mining skills and advanced modeling techniques.

Competencies themselves are nothing new. There are schools that have been delivering competency-based education offline for decades, but without a technological enabler, offline programs haven't been able to take full advantage of what competencies have to offer.

A small but growing number of educational institutions such as College for America (CfA), Brandman, Capella, University of Wisconsin, Northern Arizona, and Western Governors are implementing online competency-based programs. Although many are still in nascent stages today, it is becoming clear that online competencies have the potential to create high-quality learning pathways that are affordable, scalable, and tailored to a wide variety of industries. It is likely they will only gain traction and proliferate over time.

But this isn't vocational or career technical training nor is it the University of Phoenix. Nor is this merely about STEM-related knowledge. In fact, many of these competency-based programs have majors or a substantive core devoted to the liberal arts. And they go beyond bubble tests and machine-graded exercises. Final projects often include complex written assignments and oral presentations that demand feedback from instructors.

The key distinction is the *modularization* of learning. Nowhere else but in an online competency-based curriculum will you find this novel and flexible architecture. By breaking free of the constraints of the "course" as the educational unit, online competency-based providers can easily and cost-effectively stack together modules for various and emergent disciplines.

Here's why business leaders should care: the resulting stackable credential reveals identifiable skillsets and dispositions that *mean* something to an employer. As opposed to the black box of the diploma, competencies lead to a more transparent system that highlights student-learning outcomes.

College transcripts reveal very little about what a student knows and can do. An employer never fully knows what it means if a student got a B+ in Social Anthropology or a C- in Geology. Most colleges measure learning in credit hours, meaning that they're very good at telling you how long a student sat in a particular class—not what the student actually learned.

Competency-based learning flips this on its head and centers on mastery of a subject regardless of the time it takes to get there. A student cannot move on until demonstrating fluency in each competency. As a result, an employer can rest assured that when a student can use mathematical formulas to make financial decisions, the student has mastered that competency. Learning is fixed, and time is variable.

What's more, many of these education providers are consulting with industry councils to understand better what employers are seeking. Businesses and organizations of all sizes can help build series of brief modules to skill up their existing workforce. The bundle of modules doesn't even necessarily need to culminate in a credential or a degree because the company itself validates the learning process. Major companies like The Gap, Partners Healthcare, McDonald's, FedEx, ConAgra Foods, Delta Dental, Kawasaki, Oakley, American Hyundai, and Blizzard are just a few of the growing number of companies diving into competencies by partnering with institutions such as Brandman, CfA, and Patten. By having built that specific learning pathway in collaboration with the education provider, the employer knows that the pipeline of students will most certainly have the requisite skills for the work ahead.

For working adults who are looking to skill-up, the advantages are obvious. These programs are already priced comparable to, or lower than, community colleges, and most offer simple subscription models so students can pay a flat rate and complete as many competencies as they wish in a set time period. Instead of having to sit for 16 weeks in a single course, a student could potentially accelerate through a year's worth of learning in that same time. In fact, a student who was working full-time and enrolled at College for America earned an entire associate's degree in less than 100 days. That means fewer opportunity costs and dramatic cost savings. For some, that entire degree can be covered by an employer's tuition reimbursement program—a degree for less than $5,000. It is vital to underscore, however, that competency-based education is about mastery foremost—not speed. These pathways importantly assess and certify what a student knows and can do.

Over time, employers will be able to observe firsthand and validate whether the quality of work or outputs of their employees are markedly different with these new programs in place. Online competency-based education has the potential to provide learning experiences that drive down costs, accelerate degree completion, and produce a variety of convenient, customizable, and targeted programs for the emergent needs of our labor market.

A new world of learning lies ahead. Time to pay attention.

A Social Network Can
Be a Learning Network

DEREK BRUFF

Last fall, for my first-year writing seminar on the history and mathematics of cryptography, I posted my students' expository-writing essays on our course blog. The assignment had asked students to describe a particular code or cipher that we had not already discussed—how it came to be, how it works, how to crack it, who used it. They described more than a dozen codes and ciphers. It seemed a shame that I might be the only one to read such interesting content, so I asked the students to read and comment on two papers of their peers. The course blog provided an ideal platform for that task.

About a week later, one of my students arrived at class excited. He had Googled his paper's topic (the "Great Paris Cipher") and saw that his paper was the third result listed. He said, with a little trepidation, "Some high-school student is going to cite my paper!" Another student asked if I had seen the lengthy comment left on his blog post by a cryptography researcher he had cited. "That's pretty cool that the guy in my footnotes read my paper," he said.

Research by Richard Light, the author and Harvard University scholar, and others indicates that when students are asked to write for one another, they write more effectively. This is perhaps counterintuitive. Wouldn't students do their best work for those grading their work? But students aren't eager to be seen as poor writers by their peers, so they step up their game when writing for other students. Also, they know that their peers don't understand the course content as well as their instructors do, so they tend to provide better explanations when writing for peers.

Since my course blog was on the open Web, my students' work could

Derek Bruff is acting director of the Center for Teaching and a senior lecturer in mathematics at Vanderbilt University.

Bruff, Derek. "A Social Network Can Be a Learning Network." *The Chronicle of Higher Education.* 6 Nov. 2011. <http://chronicle.com/article/A-Social-Network-Can-Be-a/129609/>. © The Chronicle of Higher Education, Inc.

be seen by others, including Google's indexing robots and the cryptography researcher. As a result, my students ended up writing for a much bigger audience. The papers they wrote for my course weren't just academic exercises; they were authentic expressions of learning, open to the world as part of their "digital footprints."

Sharing student work on a course blog is an example of what Randall Bass and Heidi Elmendorf, of Georgetown University, call "social pedagogies." They define these as "design approaches for teaching and learning that engage students with what we might call an 'authentic audience' (other than the teacher), where the *representation of knowledge* for an audience is absolutely central to the *construction of knowledge* in a course."

I've been taken by this idea of having students create work for "authentic audiences." Some instructors have students create projects for external clients, perhaps a proposal for a local civil-engineering firm (as my Vanderbilt colleague Sanjiv Gokhale does) or a coffee-table book for an animal-rescue shelter (as does Rebecca Pope-Ruark, of Elon University). External audiences certainly motivate students to do their best work. But students can also serve as their own authentic audience when asked to create meaningful work to share with one another.

I find that the Internet makes it relatively easy to use a variety of social pedagogies. Whether you're teaching an online course or a hybrid course or just adding a few bits of online learning to a face-to-face course, you'll find many online tools that provide a natural way to tap into the motivational effects of social pedagogies to engage your students. Here are a few of them:

SOCIAL BOOKMARKING

When you save a Web site as a favorite or bookmark, it's added to a list that stays within that browser. Use another computer, and you don't have access to that bookmark. When you use a social-bookmarking service, you save your bookmarks on that server, making them available to you wherever you access the Web, and allowing you to share them with others.

Ask your students to create accounts on a social-bookmarking service and to bookmark Web sites, news articles, and other resources relevant to the course you're teaching. Create a unique "tag" for your course and have your students use it, so that their bookmarks can be easily found. Ask students to apply multiple tags to the resources they bookmark, as a way to help them locate their bookmarks quickly and to prepare them for the kind of keyword searching they'll need to do when using library databases. If you're teaching a face-to-face or hybrid class, be sure to spend some class time having students share their latest finds, so they can see the connections between this work outside class and classroom discussions.

Students most likely won't find this difficult. After all, you're asking them to surf the Web and tag pages they like. That's something they do via Facebook every day. By having them share course-related content with their peers in the class, however, you'll tap into their desires to be part of your course's learning community. And you might be surprised by the resources they find and share.

BACK CHANNELS

These days it's common for academic conferences to have back-channel conversations. While keynote speakers and session leaders are speaking, audience members are sharing highlights, asking questions, and conversing with colleagues on Twitter. Some might see this as distracting, but for many it's a form of public note-taking and active listening.

Ask your students to create accounts on Twitter or some other back-channel tool and share ideas that occur to them in your course. You might give them specific assignments, as does the University of Connecticut's Margaret Rubega, who asks students in her ornithology class to tweet about birds they see. During a face-to-face class session, you could have students discuss their reading in small groups and share observations on the back channel. Or you could simply ask them to post a single question about the week's reading they would like to discuss.

A back channel provides students a way to stay connected to the course and their fellow students. Students are often able to integrate back channels into their daily lives, checking for and sending updates on their smartphones, for instance. That helps the class become more of a community and gives students another way to learn from each other.

COLLABORATIVE DOCUMENTS

You've no doubt heard that Wikipedia is the encyclopedia that anyone can edit. Less well known is that every page in Wikipedia has a parallel discussion page, where those editing the page debate which edits to make. A Wikipedia page on a popular topic is the synthesis of dozens and sometimes hundreds of contributors, a form of peer review.

Give your students assignments in which they must collaboratively create a document. You might set up a wiki for your course, divide students into groups, and ask each group to contribute something (an essay, research report, play, etc.). Aim for your students to engage in the kind of editing and revision that you do when you write papers with colleagues. Wikis and other platforms (such as Google Docs) usually let you see what each person contributed to the project, allowing you to hold individual students accountable for their work.

Collaborative documents need not be text-based works. Sarah C. Stiles, a sociologist at Georgetown, has had her students create collaborative timelines showing the activities of characters in a text, using a presentation tool called Prezi.com. I used that tool to have my cryptography students create a map of the debate over security and privacy. They worked in small groups to brainstorm arguments, and contributed those arguments to a shared debate map synchronously during class.

Often our students engage in what Ken Bain, vice provost and a historian at Montclair State University, calls strategic or surface learning, instead of the deep learning experiences we want them to have. Deep learning is hard work, and students need to be well motivated in order to pursue it. Extrinsic factors like grades aren't sufficient—they motivate competitive students toward strategic learning and risk-averse students to surface learning.

Social pedagogies provide a way to tap into a set of intrinsic motivations that we often overlook: people's desire to be part of a community and to share what they know with that community. My students might not see the beauty and power of mathematics, but they can look forward to participating in a community effort to learn about math. Online, social pedagogies can play an important role in creating such a community. These are strong motivators, and we can make use of them in the courses we teach.

They Loved Your G.P.A.
Then They Saw Your Tweets.

NATASHA SINGER

At Bowdoin College in Brunswick, Me., admissions officers are still talking about the high school senior who attended a campus information session last year for prospective students. Throughout the presentation, she apparently posted disparaging comments on Twitter about her fellow attendees, repeatedly using a common expletive.

Perhaps she hadn't realized that colleges keep track of their social media mentions.

"It was incredibly unusual and foolish of her to do that," Scott A. Meiklejohn, Bowdoin's dean of admissions and financial aid, told me last week. The college ultimately denied the student admission, he said, because her academic record wasn't competitive. But had her credentials been better, those indiscreet posts could have scuttled her chances.

"We would have wondered about the judgment of someone who spends their time on their mobile phone and makes such awful remarks," Mr. Meiklejohn said.

As certain high school seniors work meticulously this month to finish their early applications to colleges, some may not realize that comments they casually make online could negatively affect their prospects. In fact, new research from Kaplan Test Prep, the service owned by the Washington Post Company, suggests that online scrutiny of college hopefuls is growing.

Of 381 college admissions officers who answered a Kaplan telephone questionnaire this year, 31 percent said they had visited an applicant's Facebook or other personal social media page to learn more about them—a five-percentage-point increase from last year. More crucially for those trying to get into college, 30 percent of the admissions officers said they had discovered information online that had negatively affected an applicant's prospects.

"Students' social media and digital footprint can sometimes play a role in the admissions process," says Christine Brown, the executive director of K-12 and college prep programs at Kaplan Test Prep. "It's something that is becoming more ubiquitous and less looked down upon."

In the business realm, employers now vet the online reputations of job candidates as a matter of course. Given the impulsiveness of typical teenagers, however—not to mention the already fraught nature of college acceptances and rejections—the idea that admissions officers would covertly nose around the social media posts of prospective students seems more chilling.

There is some reason for concern. Ms. Brown says that most colleges don't have formal policies about admissions officers supplementing students' files with their own online research. If colleges find seemingly troubling material online, they may not necessarily notify the applicants involved.

"To me, it's a huge problem," said Bradley S. Shear, a lawyer specializing in social media law. For one thing, Mr. Shear told me, colleges might erroneously identify the account of a person with the same name as a prospective student—or even mistake an impostor's account—as belonging to the applicant, potentially leading to unfair treatment. "Often," he added, "false and misleading content online is taken as fact."

These kinds of concerns prompted me last week to email 20 colleges and universities—small and large, private and public, East Coast and West Coast—to ask about their practices. Then I called admissions officials at 10 schools who agreed to interviews.

Each official told me that it was not routine practice at his or her institution for admissions officers to use Google searches on applicants or to peruse their social media posts. Most said their school received so many applications to review—with essays, recommendations and, often, supplemental portfolios—that staff members wouldn't be able to do extra research online. A few also felt that online investigations might lead to unfair or inconsistent treatment.

"As students' use of social media is growing, there's a whole variety of ways that college admissions officers can use it," Beth A. Wiser, the director of admissions at the University of Vermont, told me. "We have chosen to not use it as part of the process in making admissions decisions."

Other admissions officials said they did not formally prohibit the practice. In fact, they said, admissions officers did look at online material about applicants on an ad hoc basis. Sometimes prospective students themselves ask an admissions office to look at blogs or videos they have posted; on other occasions, an admissions official might look up an obscure award or event mentioned by an applicant, for purposes of elucidation.

"Last year, we watched some animation videos and we followed media stories about an applicant who was involved in a political cause," says Will Hummel, an admissions officer at Pomona College in Claremont, Calif. But those were rare instances, he says, and the supplemental material didn't significantly affect the students' admissions prospects.

Admissions officials also said they had occasionally rejected applicants, or revoked their acceptances, because of online materials. Often, these officials said, a college may learn about a potential problem from an outside source, such as a high school counselor or a graduate, prompting it to look into the matter.

Last year, an undergraduate at Pitzer College in Claremont, Calif., who had befriended a prospective student on Facebook, notified the admissions office because he noticed that the applicant had posted offensive comments about one of his high school teachers.

"We thought, this is not the kind of person we want in our community," Angel B. Perez, Pitzer's dean of admission and financial aid, told me. With about 4,200 applications annually for a first-year class of 250 students, the school can afford to be selective. "We didn't admit the student," Mr. Perez said.

But colleges vary in their transparency. While Pitzer doesn't contact students if their social media activities precluded admission to the school, Colgate University does notify students if they are eliminated from the applicant pool for any reason other than being uncompetitive candidates.

"We should be transparent with applicants," says Gary L. Ross, Colgate's dean of admission. He once called a student, to whom Colgate had already offered acceptance, to check whether an alcohol-related incident that was reported online was indeed true. (It was, and Colgate rescinded the offer of admission.)

"We will always ask if there is something we didn't understand," Mr. Ross said.

In an effort to help high school students avoid self-sabotage online, guidance counselors are tutoring them in scrubbing their digital identities. At Brookline High School in Massachusetts, juniors are taught to delete alcohol-related posts or photographs and to create socially acceptable email addresses. One junior's original email address was "bleedingjesus," said Lenny Libenzon, the school's guidance department chairman. That changed.

"They imagine admissions officers are old professors," he said. "But we tell them a lot of admissions officers are very young and technology-savvy."

Likewise, high school students seem to be growing more shrewd, changing their searchable names on Facebook or untagging themselves in pictures to obscure their digital footprints during the college admission process.

"We know that some students maintain two Facebook accounts," says Wes K. Waggoner, the dean of undergraduate admission at Southern Methodist University in Dallas.

For their part, high school seniors say that sanitizing social media accounts doesn't seem qualitatively different than the efforts they already make to present the most appealing versions of themselves to colleges. While Megan Heck, 17, a senior at East Lansing High School in Michigan, told me that she was not amending any of her posts as she applied early to colleges this month, many of her peers around the country were.

"If you've got stuff online you don't want colleges to see," Ms. Heck said, "deleting it is kind of like joining two more clubs senior year to list on your application to try to make you seem more like the person they want at their schools."

Why Free Is Not the Future of Digital Content in Education

MARY CULLINANE

As chief content Officer of a learning company, people frequently ask me: "Won't all of your content eventually be free? After all, when technology enters the market, free is right behind it."

Then they'll point to something like the music industry, where annual revenues have declined more than $20 billion from their peak over a decade ago and album sales recently hit their lowest point on record.

For $9.99 a month—less than the price of a single CD a decade ago—listeners can stream as much ad-free music as they want on Spotify, the service that made headlines in 2013 when it revealed the average payout to artists each time their songs are streamed is less than a penny. (Sorry Swifties, you now have to go to YouTube to get your "Shake It Off" fix.)

The downward price pressure exerted on the music industry (or the news business, or movies) by the digital revolution is unmistakable. But going digital will affect different industries in different ways based on market dynamics and other factors.

With music, there are characteristics about the way the user consumes the content—i.e. songs—that help explain why technology has put so much downward pressure on pricing.

For starters, the use of technology does not make me like the song itself more. It doesn't improve songs in a way that would lead me to assign additional value to them. If, like me, you're not an audiophile with an ear for the nuances of vinyl recordings, the songs are the same songs, however you play them. I appreciate the convenience of not having to cart CDs around, but in reality, the impact of this new digital use pattern on my lifestyle is minimal.

Contrast that with gaming: The video game industry has thrived

Mary Cullinane is Houghton Mifflin Harcourt's first Chief Content Officer.

in recent years. That's partly because video games provide a social experience—a service—that cannot be pirated. And technology has catalyzed this shift.

Primary and secondary education presents another case where technology fundamentally changes the way content is experienced. Just imagine: I am a teacher. I am responsible for ensuring that my students succeed in an educational process that will equip them with the knowledge and skills that are critical for their future success.

There are 30 different learning styles in my classroom and I have to reach them all. I have to be certain the resources I put in front of my students are engaging. I need a solution that allows me to understand how well they are doing, and adjust the materials they use based on their individual proficiency levels and learning progressions.

Technology helps me do this. As students engage with the content, the content learns more about the students and it also becomes "smarter". A digital engine compares students' responses to those of all other users. Equipped with that data, this adaptive learning system doesn't just show that a student answered incorrectly. It knows why she did, and uses those insights to create a customized learning path.

In doing so, technology helps solves a big problem that has always confronted teachers: students learn at different paces. Advanced students can get bored and struggling students can give up. Now, as a teacher, I can put content in front of each learner that is personalized to his or her needs. It's something teachers have been doing through the ages, but technology brings it to the next level of adaptivity.

You get the picture. In this case, technology is making educational content better. It is increasing its value. It is now able to solve a long-existing challenge. It is enabling content to do things that it could not do before. And the stakes could not be higher.

The quality of educational content has a marked impact on student achievement. If we do not get educational content right, students are less likely to gain the knowledge and skills they need to succeed in college and careers. Teachers, families, and schools need to know that the content they are using is effective, aligned to standards, and will drive student achievement.

Digital-age technology is showing up in classrooms across the United States. But that doesn't mean that "free is right behind it." High-quality content, delivered through smart digital platforms, makes it possible for teachers to work with their students in ways they never could have imagined before. And given what's at stake, that's something worth investing in.

Why Free Online Classes Are Still the Future of Education

Issie Lapowsky

The MOOC was The Next Big Thing—and then it was written off for dead. But for Anant Agarwal, one of the founding fathers of this online reboot of university education, it's only just getting started.

Agarwal is an MIT computer science professor and the CEO of the Cambridge, Massachusetts-based non-profit, edX, one of several purveyors of so-called "massively open online courses," or MOOCs, which offer free online classes from elite universities to anyone in the world. After it was buoyed by an enormous wave of hype two years ago, the MOOC has now plummeted in terms of public perception—with even one of its most prominent backers turning his back on the idea—but Agarwal is unbowed.

The way he sees it, effective uses of the MOOC model are only beginning to take shape. Enrollment in edX courses has doubled over last year, and he believes we're on the verge of an era he calls MOOC 2.0. "We've been growing as others are throwing in the towel," he says of edX.

Such optimism is to be expected from a man who makes his livelihood from this model. But Agarwal isn't alone in this opinion. This week, a team of researchers out of MIT, Harvard, and China's Tsinghua University—all schools that offer MOOCs—released a study showing that students who attended a MIT physics class online learned as effectively as students who took the class in person. What's more, the results were the same, regardless of how well the online students scored on a pre-test before taking the class.

"It's an issue that has been very controversial," said one of the study's authors, Professor David Pritchard of MIT, in a statement. "A number of well-known educators have said there isn't going to be much learning in MOOCs, or if there is, it will be for people who are already well-educated."

THE RISE AND FALL AND RISE

In 2012, *The New York Times* hailed "the year of the MOOC," and it seemed that not a day went by that there wasn't a news story about how edX—and similar companies like Coursera and Udacity–were poised to radically change and democratize education. But then came the inevitable backlash. Critics pointedly accused these companies of overstating their potential. They cited the fact that an eye-poppingly low number of students ever finish the classes as proof that the MOOC model was fundamentally broken.

Even Sebastian Thrun, founder and CEO of Udacity and one of the MOOC's earliest supporters turned his back on the model, transitioning Udacity into an online vocational school of sorts for tech companies. In an interview with *Fast Company* last fall, Thrun discussed the shift, saying: "I was realizing, we don't educate people as others wished, or as I wished. We have a lousy product."

But studies like the one from MIT are providing new fuel for people like Agarwal. It's an affirmation of the very thing they've been saying all along: that it's possible to get a quality college education without the hefty price tag. But at the same time, he says the MOOC is capable of much more. What interests Agarwal most these days are all the other, unexpected use cases for the MOOC that he and his colleagues are only beginning to discover. "There's the side of MOOCs that you see and a whole other side that you don't see," he says.

Agarwal says he was "astounded," for instance, by the fact that entire countries have begun adopting edX's open source platform, called Open edX, which allows anyone to use edX's infrastructure to launch their own MOOCs. Now, countries as diverse as France, China, and perhaps most surprisingly, Saudi Arabia, have launched national education platforms powered by edX. In Saudi Arabia, the Ministry of Labor is using Open edX to educate more women, disabled citizens, and people living in rural areas. "This is something I could not have dreamed about," Agarwal says.

BIG MOOC ON CAMPUS

In addition to connecting people to education online, MOOCs are also starting to find their way on campus, as universities like MIT and others are adopting what's known as a blended learning model. In a blended learning environment, students receive most of their lectures by video so they can spend class time doing hands-on work. At MIT, Agarwal says, two out of every three undergrads use edX as part of their on-campus courses.

Another unintended consequence of MOOCs is the massive amount of data they produce on how people learn best. EdX has found, for instance, that the longer a video lecture runs, the less time students spend watching it. So if a video lasts 40 minutes, students may only watch it for 2. If it's 6 minutes long, they'll watch the whole thing.

Such insight questions the very format of the college lecture, which often involves a professor pontificating on a topic for an hour or more. "It says learners want to learn in bite-sized chunks," he says. Now, edX has even launched A/B testing on its site, allowing professors to try out different methods of teaching and comparing student outcomes. "It's how a professor can begin to learn what's working and what's not working and have a process for improving the course," he says.

More recently, edX found yet another application for its courses: college prep. In an effort to cut their budgets, school districts across the country have cancelled advanced placement courses, even as students increasingly look to those courses as a way to cut down on college tuition costs. EdX is now hoping to fill that gap by allowing students to take those courses online.

Not only that, but edX is also offering courses in college admissions guidance, where students and parents can learn about things like attaining financial aid and writing a college essay. Such skills have also become casualties of budget cuts, as schools reduce the number of guidance counselors on staff. "Now you don't have to have a rich school district to get good guidance," Agarwal says.

LET'S NOT GO TOO FAR

Of course, MOOCs are not without their flaws. Agarwal admits that as long as MOOCs are free—and they probably always will be—low completion rates will persist. And as long as there are lousy teachers—and there probably always will be—there will be lousy courses.

But to condemn the entire model for these kinks would be like condemning Uber for the possibility of getting a bad driver or Airbnb for the chance that a guest might trash your house. These companies needed the freedom to figure out how to deal with these issues.

Perhaps more importantly, they needed the space to figure out what purpose they really serve. It's that kind of patience that's allowed Uber to grow from a taxi service to an on-demand delivery giant, and enabled

Airbnb to transform itself into a full-scale hospitality brand, not simply a tool for finding a cheap couch to crash on. To judge a breakthrough technology by only its earliest flaws is to ignore all the good it might do when given the time and the trust to do it.

Politics

Is Google Making Us Stupid?

NICHOLAS CARR

Dave, stop. Stop, will you? Stop, Dave. Will you stop, Dave?" So the supercomputer HAL pleads with the implacable astronaut Dave Bowman in a famous and weirdly poignant scene toward the end of Stanley Kubrick's *2001: A Space Odyssey*. Bowman, having nearly been sent to a deep-space death by the malfunctioning machine, is calmly, coldly disconnecting the memory circuits that control its artificial " brain. "Dave, my mind is going," HAL says, forlornly. "I can feel it. I can feel it."

I can feel it, too. Over the past few years I've had an uncomfortable sense that someone, or something, has been tinkering with my brain, remapping the neural circuitry, reprogramming the memory. My mind isn't going—so far as I can tell—but it's changing. I'm not thinking the way I used to think. I can feel it most strongly when I'm reading. Immersing myself in a book or a lengthy article used to be easy. My mind would get caught up in the narrative or the turns of the argument, and I'd spend hours strolling through long stretches of prose. That's rarely the case anymore. Now my concentration often starts to drift after two or three pages. I get fidgety, lose the thread, begin looking for something else to do. I feel as if I'm always dragging my wayward brain back to the text. The deep reading that used to come naturally has become a struggle.

I think I know what's going on. For more than a decade now, I've been spending a lot of time online, searching and surfing and sometimes adding to the great databases of the Internet. The Web has been a godsend to me as a writer. Research that once required days in the stacks or periodical rooms of libraries can now be done in minutes. A few Google searches, some quick clicks on hyperlinks, and I've got the telltale fact or pithy quote I was after. Even when I'm not working, I'm as likely as not to be foraging in the Web's info-thickets, reading and writing e-mails, scanning headlines and blog posts, watching videos and listening to podcasts, or just tripping from link to link to link. (Unlike footnotes, to

Carr, Nicholas. "Is Google Making Us Stupid?" *The Atlantic*. July/Aug. 2008. Web. 12 Mar. 2011. © Atlantic Media, Inc.

which they're sometimes likened, hyperlinks don't merely point to related works; they propel you toward them.)

For me, as for others, the Net is becoming a universal medium, the conduit for most of the information that flows through my eyes and ears and into my mind. The advantages of having immediate access to such an incredibly rich store of information are many, and they've been widely described and duly applauded. "The perfect recall of silicon memory," *Wired's* Clive Thompson has written, "can be an enormous boon to thinking." But that boon comes at a price. As the media theorist Marshall McLuhan pointed out in the 1960s, media are not just passive channels of information. They supply the stuff of thought, but they also shape the process of thought. And what the Net seems to be doing is chipping away my capacity for concentration and contemplation. My mind now expects to take in information the way the Net distributes it: in a swiftly moving stream of particles. Once I was a scuba diver in the sea of words. Now I zip along the surface like a guy on a Jet Ski.

I'm not the only one. When I mention my troubles with reading to friends and acquaintances—literary types, most of them—many say they're having similar experiences. The more they use the Web, the more they have to fight to stay focused on long pieces of writing. Some of the bloggers I follow have also begun mentioning the phenomenon. Scott Karp, who writes a blog about online media, recently confessed that he has stopped reading books altogether. "I was a lit major in college, and used to be [a] voracious book reader," he wrote. "What happened?" He speculates on the answer: "What if I do all my reading on the web not so much because the way I read has changed, i.e. I'm just seeking convenience, but because the way I THINK has changed?"

Bruce Friedman, who blogs regularly about the use of computers in medicine, also has described how the Internet has altered his mental habits. "I now have almost totally lost the ability to read and absorb a longish article on the web or in print," he wrote earlier this year. A pathologist who has long been on the faculty of the University of Michigan Medical School, Friedman elaborated on his comment in a telephone conversation with me. His thinking, he said, has taken on a "staccato" quality, reflecting the way he quickly scans short passages of text from many sources online. "I can't read *War and Peace* anymore," he admitted. "I've lost the ability to do that. Even a blog post of more than three or four paragraphs is too much to absorb. I skim it."

Anecdotes alone don't prove much. And we still await the long-term neurological and psychological experiments that will provide a definitive picture of how Internet use affects cognition. But a recently published study of online research habits , conducted by scholars from University College London, suggests that we may well be in the midst of a sea change in the way we read and think. As part of the five-year research program, the scholars examined computer logs documenting the behavior of visitors to two popular research sites, one operated by the British Library and one by a U.K. educational consortium, that provide access to journal articles, e-books, and other sources of written information. They found that people using the sites exhibited "a form of skimming activity," hopping from one source to another and rarely returning to any source they'd already visited. They typically read no more than one or two pages of an article or book before they would "bounce" out to another site. Sometimes they'd save a long article, but there's no evidence that they ever went back and actually read it. The authors of the study report:

> It is clear that users are not reading online in the traditional sense; indeed there are signs that new forms of "reading" are emerging as users "power browse" horizontally through titles, contents pages, and abstracts going for quick wins. It almost seems that they go online to avoid reading in the traditional sense.

Thanks to the ubiquity of text on the Internet, not to mention the popularity of text-messaging on cell phones, we may well be reading more today than we did in the 1970s or 1980s, when television was our medium of choice. But it's a different kind of reading, and behind it lies a different kind of thinking—perhaps even a new sense of the self. "We are not only what we read," says Maryanne Wolf, a developmental psychologist at Tufts University and the author of *Proust and the Squid: The Story and Science of the Reading Brain.* "We are how we read." Wolf worries that the style of reading promoted by the Net, a style that puts "efficiency" and "immediacy" above all else, may be weakening our capacity for the kind of deep reading that emerged when an earlier technology, the printing press, made long and complex works of prose commonplace. When we read online, she says, we tend to become "mere decoders of information." Our ability to interpret text, to make the rich mental connections that form when we read deeply and without distraction, remains largely disengaged.

Reading, explains Wolf, is not an instinctive skill for human beings. It's not etched into our genes the way speech is. We have to teach our minds how to translate the symbolic characters we see into the language we understand. And the media or other technologies we use in learning and practicing the craft of reading play an important part in shaping the neural circuits inside our brains. Experiments demonstrate that readers of ideograms, such as the Chinese, develop a mental circuitry for reading that is very different from the circuitry found in those of us whose written language employs an alphabet. The variations extend across many regions of the brain, including those that govern such essential cognitive functions as memory and the interpretation of visual and auditory stimuli. We can expect as well that the circuits woven by our use of the Net will be different from those woven by our reading of books and other printed works.

Sometime in 1882, Friedrich Nietzsche bought a typewriter—a Malling-Hansen Writing Ball, to be precise. His vision was failing, and keeping his eyes focused on a page had become exhausting and painful, often bringing on crushing headaches. He had been forced to curtail his writing, and he feared that he would soon have to give it up. The typewriter rescued him, at least for a time. Once he had mastered touch-typing, he was able to write with his eyes closed, using only the tips of his fingers. Words could once again flow from his mind to the page.

But the machine had a subtler effect on his work. One of Nietzsche's friends, a composer, noticed a change in the style of his writing. His already terse prose had become even tighter, more telegraphic. "Perhaps you will through this instrument even take to a new idiom," the friend wrote in a letter, noting that, in his own work, his "'thoughts in music and language often depend on the quality of pen and paper."

"You are right," Nietzsche replied, "our writing equipment takes part in the forming of our thoughts." Under the sway of the machine, writes the German media scholar Friedrich A. Kittler , Nietzsche's prose "changed from arguments to aphorisms, from thoughts to puns, from rhetoric to telegram style."

The human brain is almost infinitely malleable. People used to think that our mental meshwork, the dense connections formed among the 100 billion or so neurons inside our skulls, was largely fixed by the time we reached adulthood. But brain researchers have discovered that that's not the case. James Olds, a professor of neuroscience who directs the Krasnow Institute for Advanced Study at George Mason University, says that even the adult mind "is very plastic." Nerve cells routinely break old connections and form new ones. "The brain," according to Olds, "has the ability to reprogram itself on the fly, altering the way it functions."

As we use what the sociologist Daniel Bell has called our "intellectual technologies"—the tools that extend our mental rather than our physical capacities—we inevitably begin to take on the qualities of those technologies. The mechanical clock, which came into common use in the 14th century, provides a compelling example. In *Technics and Civilization,* the historian and cultural critic Lewis Mumford described how the clock "disassociated time from human events and helped create the belief in an independent world of mathematically measurable sequences." The "abstract framework of divided time" became "the point of reference for both action and thought."

The clock's methodical ticking helped bring into being the scientific mind and the scientific man. But it also took something away. As the late MIT computer scientist Joseph Weizenbaum observed in his 1976 book, *Computer Power and Human Reason: From Judgment to Calculation,* the conception of the world that emerged from the widespread use of time-keeping instruments "remains an impoverished version of the older one, for it rests on a rejection of those direct experiences that formed the basis for, and indeed constituted, the old reality." In deciding when to eat, to work, to sleep, to rise, we stopped listening to our senses and started obeying the clock.

The process of adapting to new intellectual technologies is reflected in the changing metaphors we use to explain ourselves to ourselves. When the mechanical clock arrived, people began thinking of their brains as operating "like clockwork." Today, in the age of software, we have come to think of them as operating "like computers." But the changes, neuroscience tells us, go much deeper than metaphor. Thanks to our brain's plasticity, the adaptation occurs also at a biological level.

The Internet promises to have particularly far-reaching effects on cognition. In a paper published in 1936, the British mathematician Alan Turing proved that a digital computer, which at the time existed only as a theoretical machine, could be programmed to perform the function of any other information-processing device. And that's what we're seeing today. The Internet, an immeasurably powerful computing system, is subsuming most of our other intellectual technologies. It's becoming our map and our clock, our printing press and our typewriter, our calculator and our telephone, and our radio and TV.

When the Net absorbs a medium, that medium is re-created in the Net's image. It injects the medium's content with hyperlinks, blinking ads, and other digital gewgaws, and it surrounds the content with the content of all the other media it has absorbed. A new e-mail message, for instance, may announce its arrival as we're glancing over the latest headlines at a newspaper's site. The result is to scatter our attention and diffuse our concentration.

The Net's influence doesn't end at the edges of a computer screen, either. As people's minds become attuned to the crazy quilt of Internet media, traditional media have to adapt to the audience's new expectations. Television programs add text crawls and pop-up ads, and magazines and newspapers shorten their articles, introduce capsule summaries, and crowd their pages with easy-to-browse info-snippets. When, in March of this year, *The New York Times* decided to devote the second and third pages of every edition to article abstracts , its design director, Tom Bodkin, explained that the "shortcuts" would give harried readers a quick "taste" of the day's news, sparing them the "less efficient" method of actually turning the pages and reading the articles. Old media have little choice but to play by the new-media rules.

Never has a communications system played so many roles in our lives—or exerted such broad influence over our thoughts—as the Internet does today. Yet, for all that's been written about the Net, there's been little consideration of how, exactly, it's reprogramming us. The Net's intellectual ethic remains obscure.

About the same time that Nietzsche started using his typewriter, an earnest young man named Frederick Winslow Taylor carried a stopwatch into the Midvale Steel plant in Philadelphia and began a historic series of experiments aimed at improving the efficiency of the plant's machinists. With the approval of Midvale's owners, he recruited a group of factory hands, set them to work on various metalworking machines, and recorded and timed their every movement as well as the operations of the machines. By breaking down every job into a sequence of small, discrete steps and then testing different ways of performing each one, Taylor created a set of precise instructions—an "algorithm," we might say today—for how each worker should work. Midvale's employees grumbled about the strict new regime, claiming that it turned them into little more than automatons, but the factory's productivity soared.

More than a hundred years after the invention of the steam engine, the Industrial Revolution had at last found its philosophy and its philosopher. Taylor's tight industrial choreography—his "system," as he liked to call it—was embraced by manufacturers throughout the country and, in time, around the world. Seeking maximum speed, maximum efficiency, and maximum output, factory owners used time-and-motion studies to organize their work and configure the jobs of their workers. The goal, as Taylor defined it in his celebrated 1911 treatise, *The Principles of Scientific Management,* was to identify and adopt, for every job, the "one best method" of work and thereby to effect "the gradual substitution of science for rule of thumb throughout the mechanic arts." Once his system was applied to all acts of manual labor, Taylor assured his followers, it would bring about a restructuring not only of industry but of society, creating a utopia of perfect efficiency. "In the past the man has been first," he declared; "in the future the system must be first."

Taylor's system is still very much with us; it remains the ethic of industrial manufacturing. And now, thanks to the growing power that computer engineers and software coders wield over our intellectual lives, Taylor's ethic is beginning to govern the realm of the mind as well. The Internet is a machine designed for the efficient and automated collection, transmission, and manipulation of information, and its legions of programmers are intent on finding the "one best method"—the perfect algorithm—to carry out every mental movement of what we've come to describe as "knowledge work."

Google's headquarters, in Mountain View, California—the Googleplex—is the Internet's high church, and the religion practiced inside its walls is Taylorism. Google, says its chief executive, Eric Schmidt, is "a company that's founded around the science of measurement," and it is striving to "systematize everything" it does. Drawing on the terabytes of behavioral data it collects through its search engine and other sites, it carries out thousands of experiments a day, according to the *Harvard Business Review,* and it uses the results to refine the algorithms that increasingly control how people find information and extract meaning from it. What Taylor did for the work of the hand, Google is doing for the work of the mind.

The company has declared that its mission is "to organize the world's information and make it universally accessible and useful." It seeks to develop "the perfect search engine," which it defines as something that "understands exactly what you mean and gives you back exactly what you want." In Google's view, information is a kind of commodity, a utilitarian resource that can be mined and processed with industrial efficiency. The more pieces of information we can "access" and the faster we can extract their gist, the more productive we become as thinkers.

Where does it end? Sergey Brin and Larry Page, the gifted young men who founded Google while pursuing doctoral degrees in computer science at Stanford, speak frequently of their desire to turn their search engine into an artificial intelligence, a HAL-like machine that might be connected directly to our brains. "The ultimate search engine is something as smart as people—or smarter," Page said in a speech a few years back. "For us, working on search is a way to work on artificial intelligence." In a 2004 interview with *Newsweek,* Brin said, "Certainly if you had all the world's information directly attached to your brain, or an artificial brain that was smarter than your brain, you'd be better off." Last year, Page told a convention of scientists that Google is "really trying to build artificial intelligence and to do it on a large scale."

Such an ambition is a natural one, even an admirable one, for a pair of math whizzes with vast quantities of cash at their disposal and a small army of computer scientists in their employ. A fundamentally scientific enterprise, Google is motivated by a desire to use technology, in Eric Schmidt's words, "to solve problems that have never been solved before," and artificial intelligence is the hardest problem out there. Why wouldn't Brin and Page want to be the ones to crack it?

Still, their easy assumption that we'd all "be better off" if our brains were supplemented, or even replaced, by an artificial intelligence is unsettling. It suggests a belief that intelligence is the output of a mechanical process, a series of discrete steps that can be isolated, measured, and optimized. In Google's world, the world we enter when we go online, there's little place for the fuzziness of contemplation. Ambiguity is not an opening for insight but a bug to be fixed. The human brain is just an outdated computer that needs a faster processor and a bigger hard drive.

The idea that our minds should operate as high-speed data-processing machines is not only built into the workings of the Internet, it is the network's reigning business model as well. The faster we surf across the Web—the more links we click and pages we view—the more opportunities Google and other companies gain to collect information about us and to feed us advertisements. Most of the proprietors of the commercial Internet have a financial stake in collecting the crumbs of data we leave behind as we flit from link to link—the more crumbs, the better. The last thing these companies want is to encourage leisurely reading or slow, concentrated thought. It's in their economic interest to drive us to distraction.

Maybe I'm just a worrywart. Just as there's a tendency to glorify technological progress, there's a countertendency to expect the worst of every new tool or machine. In Plato's *Phaedrus,* Socrates bemoaned the development of writing. He feared that, as people came to rely on the written word as a substitute for the knowledge they used to carry inside their heads, they would, in the words of one of the dialogue's characters, "cease to exercise their memory and become forgetful." And because they would be able to "receive a quantity of information without proper instruction," they would "be thought very knowledgeable when they are for the most part quite ignorant." They would be "filled with the conceit of wisdom instead of real wisdom." Socrates wasn't wrong—the new technology did often have the effects he feared—but he was shortsighted. He couldn't foresee the many ways that writing and reading would serve to spread information, spur fresh ideas, and expand human knowledge (if not wisdom).

The arrival of Gutenberg's printing press, in the 15th century, set off another round of teeth gnashing. The Italian humanist Hieronimo Squarciafico worried that the easy availability of books would lead to intellectual laziness, making men "less studious" and weakening their minds. Others argued that cheaply printed books and broadsheets would undermine religious authority, demean the work of scholars and scribes, and spread sedition and debauchery. As New York University professor Clay Shirky notes, "Most of the arguments made against the printing press were correct, even prescient." But, again, the doomsayers were unable to imagine the myriad blessings that the printed word would deliver.

So, yes, you should be skeptical of my skepticism. Perhaps those who dismiss critics of the Internet as Luddites or nostalgists will be proved correct, and from our hyperactive, data-stoked minds will spring a golden age of intellectual discovery and universal wisdom. Then again, the Net isn't the alphabet, and although it may replace the printing press, it produces something altogether different. The kind of deep reading that a sequence of printed pages promotes is valuable not just for the knowledge we acquire from the author's words but for the intellectual vibrations those words set off within our own minds. In the quiet spaces opened up by the sustained, undistracted reading of a book, or by any other act of contemplation, for that matter, we make our own associations, draw our own inferences and analogies, foster our own ideas. Deep reading, as Maryanne Wolf argues, is indistinguishable from deep thinking.

If we lose those quiet spaces, or fill them up with "content," we will sacrifice something important not only in our selves but in our culture. In a recent essay, the playwright Richard Foreman eloquently described what's at stake:

I come from a tradition of Western culture, in which the

ideal (my ideal) was the complex, dense and "cathedral-like" structure of the highly educated and articulate personality—a man or woman who carried inside themselves a personally constructed and unique version of the entire heritage of the West. [But now] I see within us all (myself included) the replacement of complex inner density with a new kind of self—evolving under the pressure of information overload and the technology of the "instantly available."

As we are drained of our "inner repertory of dense cultural inheritance," Foreman concluded, we risk turning into "'pancake people'— spread wide and thin as we connect with that vast network of information accessed by the mere touch of a button."

I'm haunted by that scene in *2001*. What makes it so poignant, and so weird, is the computer's emotional response to the disassembly of its mind: its despair as one circuit after another goes dark, its childlike pleading with the astronaut—"I can feel it. I can feel it. I'm afraid"—and its final reversion to what can only be called a state of innocence. HAL's outpouring of feeling contrasts with the emotionlessness that characterizes the human figures in the film, who go about their business with an almost robotic efficiency. Their thoughts and actions feel scripted, as if they're following the steps of an algorithm. In the world of *2001,* people have become so machinelike that the most human character turns out to be a machine. That's the essence of Kubrick's dark prophecy: as we come to rely on computers to mediate our understanding of the world, it is our own intelligence that flattens into artificial intelligence.

Small Change: Why the Revolution Will Not Be Tweeted

MALCOLM GLADWELL

At four-thirty in the afternoon on Monday, February 1, 1960, four college students sat down at the lunch counter at the Woolworth's in downtown Greensboro, North Carolina. They were freshmen at North Carolina A. & T., a black college a mile or so away.

"I'd like a cup of coffee, please," one of the four, Ezell Blair, said to the waitress.

"We don't serve Negroes here," she replied.

The Woolworth's lunch counter was a long L-shaped bar that could seat sixty-six people, with a standup snack bar at one end. The seats were for whites. The snack bar was for blacks. Another employee, a black woman who worked at the steam table, approached the students and tried to warn them away. "You're acting stupid, ignorant!" she said. They didn't move. Around five-thirty, the front doors to the store were locked. The four still didn't move. Finally, they left by a side door. Outside, a small crowd had gathered, including a photographer from the Greensboro *Record*. "I'll be back tomorrow with A. & T. College," one of the students said.

By next morning, the protest had grown to twenty-seven men and four women, most from the same dormitory as the original four. The men were dressed in suits and ties. The students had brought their schoolwork, and studied as they sat at the counter. On Wednesday, students from Greensboro's "Negro" secondary school, Dudley High, joined in, and the number of protesters swelled to eighty. By Thursday, the protesters numbered three hundred, including three white women, from the Greensboro campus of the University of North Carolina. By Saturday, the sit-in had reached six hundred. People spilled out onto the street. White teen-agers waved Confederate flags. Someone threw a firecracker. At noon, the

Gladwell, Malcolm. "Small Change: Why the Revolution Will Not Be Tweeted." *The New Yorker.* 4 Oct. 2010. Web. 13 Mar. 2011. © Conde Nast Publications, Inc.

A. & T. football team arrived. "Here comes the wrecking crew," one of the white students shouted.[1]

By the following Monday, sit-ins had spread to Winston-Salem, twenty-five miles away, and Durham, fifty miles away. The day after that, students at Fayetteville State Teachers College and at Johnson C. Smith College, in Charlotte, joined in, followed on Wednesday by students at St. Augustine's College and Shaw University, in Raleigh. On Thursday and Friday, the protest crossed state lines, surfacing in Hampton and Portsmouth, Virginia, in Rock Hill, South Carolina, and in Chattanooga, Tennessee. By the end of the month, there were sit-ins throughout the South, as far west as Texas. "I asked every student I met what the first day of the sitdowns had been like on his campus," the political theorist Michael Walzer wrote in *Dissent*. "The answer was always the same: 'It was like a fever. Everyone wanted to go.'" Some seventy thousand students eventually took part. Thousands were arrested and untold thousands more radicalized. These events in the early sixties became a civil-rights war that engulfed the South for the rest of the decade—and it happened without e-mail, texting, Facebook, or Twitter.

The world, we are told, is in the midst of a revolution. The new tools of social media have reinvented social activism. With Facebook and Twitter and the like, the traditional relationship between political authority and popular will has been upended, making it easier for the powerless to collaborate, coordinate, and give voice to their concerns. When ten thousand protesters took to the streets in Moldova in the spring of 2009 to protest against their country's Communist government, the action was dubbed the Twitter Revolution, because of the means by which the demonstrators had been brought together. A few months after that, when student protests rocked Tehran, the State Department took the unusual step of asking Twitter to suspend scheduled maintenance of its Web site, because the Administration didn't want such a critical organizing tool out of service at the height of the demonstrations. "Without Twitter the people of Iran would not have felt empowered and confident to stand up for freedom and democracy," Mark Pfeifle, a former national-security adviser, later wrote, calling for Twitter to be nominated for the Nobel Peace Prize. Where activists were once defined by their causes, they are now defined by their tools. Facebook warriors go online to push for change. "You are the best hope for us all," James K. Glassman, a former senior State Depart-

---

1 Clarification: This piece's account of the Greensboro sit-in comes from Miles Wolff's "Lunch at the Five and Ten" (1970).

ment official, told a crowd of cyber activists at a recent conference sponsored by Facebook, A. T. & T., Howcast, MTV, and Google. Sites like Facebook, Glassman said, "give the U.S. a significant competitive advantage over terrorists. Some time ago, I said that Al Qaeda was 'eating our lunch on the Internet.' That is no longer the case. Al Qaeda is stuck in Web 1.0. The Internet is now about interactivity and conversation."

These are strong, and puzzling, claims. Why does it matter who is eating whose lunch on the Internet? Are people who log on to their Facebook page really the best hope for us all? As for Moldova's so-called Twitter Revolution, Evgeny Morozov, a scholar at Stanford who has been the most persistent of digital evangelism's critics, points out that Twitter had scant internal significance in Moldova, a country where very few Twitter accounts exist. Nor does it seem to have been a revolution, not least because the protests—as Anne Applebaum suggested in the *Washington Post*—may well have been a bit of stagecraft cooked up by the government. (In a country paranoid about Romanian revanchism, the protesters flew a Romanian flag over the Parliament building.) In the Iranian case, meanwhile, the people tweeting about the demonstrations were almost all in the West. "It is time to get Twitter's role in the events in Iran right," Golnaz Esfandiari wrote, this past summer, in *Foreign Policy*. "Simply put: There was no Twitter Revolution inside Iran." The cadre of prominent bloggers, like Andrew Sullivan, who championed the role of social media in Iran, Esfandiari continued, misunderstood the situation. "Western journalists who couldn't reach—or didn't bother reaching?—people on the ground in Iran simply scrolled through the English-language tweets post with tag #iranelection," she wrote. "Through it all, no one seemed to wonder why people trying to coordinate protests in Iran would be writing in any language other than Farsi."

Some of this grandiosity is to be expected. Innovators tend to be solipsists. They often want to cram every stray fact and experience into their new model. As the historian Robert Darnton has written, "The marvels of communication technology in the present have produced a false consciousness about the past—even a sense that communication has no history, or had nothing of importance to consider before the days of television and the Internet." But there is something else at work here, in the outsized enthusiasm for social media. Fifty years after one of the most extraordinary episodes of social upheaval in American history, we seem to have forgotten what activism is.

Greensboro in the early nineteen-sixties was the kind of place where racial insubordination was routinely met with violence. The four students who first sat down at the lunch counter were terrified. "I suppose if anyone had come up behind me and yelled 'Boo,' I think I would have fallen off my seat," one of them said later. On the first day, the store manager notified the police chief, who immediately sent two officers to the store. On the third day, a gang of white toughs showed up at the lunch counter and stood ostentatiously behind the protesters, ominously muttering epithets such as "burr-head nigger." A local Ku Klux Klan leader made an appearance. On Saturday, as tensions grew, someone called in a bomb threat, and the entire store had to be evacuated.

The dangers were even clearer in the Mississippi Freedom Summer Project of 1964, another of the sentinel campaigns of the civil-rights movement. The Student Nonviolent Coordinating Committee recruited hundreds of Northern, largely white unpaid volunteers to run Freedom Schools, register black voters, and raise civil-rights awareness in the Deep South. "No one should go *anywhere* alone, but certainly not in an automobile and certainly not at night," they were instructed. Within days of arriving in Mississippi, three volunteers—Michael Schwerner, James Chaney, and Andrew Goodman—were kidnapped and killed, and, during the rest of the summer, thirty-seven black churches were set on fire and dozens of safe houses were bombed; volunteers were beaten, shot at, arrested, and trailed by pickup trucks full of armed men. A quarter of those in the program dropped out. Activism that challenges the status quo—that attacks deeply rooted problems—is not for the faint of heart.

What makes people capable of this kind of activism? The Stanford sociologist Doug McAdam compared the Freedom Summer dropouts with the participants who stayed, and discovered that the key difference wasn't, as might be expected, ideological fervor. "*All* of the applicants—participants and withdrawals alike—emerge as highly committed, articulate supporters of the goals and values of the summer program," he concluded. What mattered more was an applicant's degree of personal connection to the civil-rights movement. All the volunteers were required to provide a list of personal contacts—the people they wanted kept apprised of their activities—and participants were far more likely than dropouts to have close friends who were also going to Mississippi. High-risk activism, McAdam concluded, is a "strong-tie" phenomenon.

This pattern shows up again and again. One study of the Red Brigades, the Italian terrorist group of the nineteen-seventies, found that seventy per cent of recruits had at least one good friend already in the organization. The same is true of the men who joined the mujahideen in Afghanistan. Even revolutionary actions that look spontaneous, like the demonstrations in East Germany that led to the fall of the Berlin Wall, are, at core, strong-tie phenomena. The opposition movement in East Germany consisted of several hundred groups, each with roughly a dozen members. Each group was in limited contact with the others: at the time, only thirteen per cent of East Germans even had a phone. All they knew was that on Monday nights, outside St. Nicholas Church in downtown Leipzig, people gathered to voice their anger at the state. And the primary determinant of who showed up was "critical friends"—the more friends you had who were critical of the regime the more likely you were to join the protest.

So one crucial fact about the four freshmen at the Greensboro lunch counter—David Richmond, Franklin McCain, Ezell Blair, and Joseph McNeil—was their relationship with one another. McNeil was a room-mate of Blair's in A. & T.'s Scott Hall dormitory. Richmond roomed with McCain one floor up, and Blair, Richmond, and McCain had all gone to Dudley High School. The four would smuggle beer into the dorm and talk late into the night in Blair and McNeil's room. They would all have remembered the murder of Emmett Till in 1955, the Montgomery bus boycott that same year, and the showdown in Little Rock in 1957. It was McNeil who brought up the idea of a sit-in at Woolworth's. They'd dis-cussed it for nearly a month. Then McNeil came into the dorm room and asked the others if they were ready. There was a pause, and McCain said, in a way that works only with people who talk late into the night with one another, "Are you guys chicken or not?" Ezell Blair worked up the courage the next day to ask for a cup of coffee because he was flanked by his room-mate and two good friends from high school.

The kind of activism associated with social media isn't like this at all. The platforms of social media are built around weak ties. Twitter is a way of following (or being followed by) people you may never have met. Face-book is a tool for efficiently managing your acquaintances, for keeping up with the people you would not otherwise be able to stay in touch with. That's why you can have a thousand "friends" on Facebook, as you never could in real life.

This is in many ways a wonderful thing. There is strength in weak ties, as the sociologist Mark Granovetter has observed. Our acquaintances—not our friends—are our greatest source of new ideas and information. The Internet lets us exploit the power of these kinds of distant connections with marvelous efficiency. It's terrific at the diffusion of innovation, interdisciplinary collaboration, seamlessly matching up buyers and sellers, and the logistical functions of the dating world. But weak ties seldom lead to high-risk activism.

In a new book called "The Dragonfly Effect: Quick, Effective, and Powerful Ways to Use Social Media to Drive Social Change," the business consultant Andy Smith and the Stanford Business School professor Jennifer Aaker tell the story of Sameer Bhatia, a young Silicon Valley entrepreneur who came down with acute myelogenous leukemia. It's a perfect illustration of social media's strengths. Bhatia needed a bone-marrow transplant, but he could not find a match among his relatives and friends. The odds were best with a donor of his ethnicity, and there were few South Asians in the national bone-marrow database. So Bhatia's business partner sent out an e-mail explaining Bhatia's plight to more than four hundred of their acquaintances, who forwarded the e-mail to their personal contacts; Facebook pages and YouTube videos were devoted to the Help Sameer campaign. Eventually, nearly twenty-five thousand new people were registered in the bone-marrow database, and Bhatia found a match.

But how did the campaign get so many people to sign up? By not asking too much of them. That's the only way you can get someone you don't really know to do something on your behalf. You can get thousands of people to sign up for a donor registry, because doing so is pretty easy. You have to send in a cheek swab and—in the highly unlikely event that your bone marrow is a good match for someone in need—spend a few hours at the hospital. Donating bone marrow isn't a trivial matter. But it doesn't involve financial or personal risk; it doesn't mean spending a summer being chased by armed men in pickup trucks. It doesn't require that you confront socially entrenched norms and practices. In fact, it's the kind of commitment that will bring only social acknowledgment and praise.

The evangelists of social media don't understand this distinction; they seem to believe that a Facebook friend is the same as a real friend and that signing up for a donor registry in Silicon Valley today is activism in the same sense as sitting at a segregated lunch counter in Greensboro in 1960. "Social networks are particularly effective at increasing motivation," Aaker and Smith write. But that's not true. Social networks are effective at increasing *participation*—by lessening the level of motivation that participation requires. The Facebook page of the Save Darfur Coalition has 1,282,339 members, who have donated an average of nine cents apiece.

The next biggest Darfur charity on Facebook has 22,073 members, who have donated an average of thirty-five cents. Help Save Darfur has 2,797 members, who have given, on average, fifteen cents. A spokesperson for the Save Darfur Coalition told *Newsweek,* "We wouldn't necessarily gauge someone's value to the advocacy movement based on what they've given. This is a powerful mechanism to engage this critical population. They inform their community, attend events, volunteer. It's not something you can measure by looking at a ledger." In other words, Facebook activism succeeds not by motivating people to make a real sacrifice but by motivating them to do the things that people do when they are not motivated enough to make a real sacrifice. We are a long way from the lunch counters of Greensboro.

The students who joined the sit-ins across the South during the winter of 1960 described the movement as a "fever." But the civil-rights movement was more like a military campaign than like a contagion. In the late nineteen-fifties, there had been sixteen sit-ins in various cities throughout the South, fifteen of which were formally organized by civil-rights organizations like the N.A.A.C.P. and CORE. Possible locations for activism were scouted. Plans were drawn up. Movement activists held training sessions and retreats for would-be protesters. The Greensboro Four were a product of this groundwork: all were members of the N.A.A.C.P. Youth Council. They had close ties with the head of the local N.A.A.C.P. chapter. They had been briefed on the earlier wave of sit-ins in Durham, and had been part of a series of movement meetings in activist churches. When the sit-in movement spread from Greensboro throughout the South, it did not spread indiscriminately. It spread to those cities which had preexisting "movement centers"—a core of dedicated and trained activists ready to turn the "fever" into action.

The civil-rights movement was high-risk activism. It was also, crucially, strategic activism: a challenge to the establishment mounted with precision and discipline. The N.A.A.C.P. was a centralized organization, run from New York according to highly formalized operating procedures. At the Southern Christian Leadership Conference, Martin Luther King, Jr., was the unquestioned authority. At the center of the movement was the black church, which had, as Aldon D. Morris points out in his superb 1984 study, "The Origins of the Civil Rights Movement," a carefully demarcated division of labor, with various standing committees and disciplined groups. "Each group was task-oriented and coordinated its activities through authority structures," Morris writes. "Individuals were held accountable for their assigned duties, and important conflicts were resolved by the minister, who usually exercised ultimate authority over the congregation."

This is the second crucial distinction between traditional activism and its online variant: social media are not about this kind of hierarchical organization. Facebook and the like are tools for building *networks,* which are the opposite, in structure and character, of hierarchies. Unlike hierarchies, with their rules and procedures, networks aren't controlled by a single central authority. Decisions are made through consensus, and the ties that bind people to the group are loose.

This structure makes networks enormously resilient and adaptable in low-risk situations. Wikipedia is a perfect example. It doesn't have an editor, sitting in New York, who directs and corrects each entry. The effort of putting together each entry is self-organized. If every entry in Wikipedia were to be erased tomorrow, the content would swiftly be restored, because that's what happens when a network of thousands spontaneously devote their time to a task.

There are many things, though, that networks don't do well. Car companies sensibly use a network to organize their hundreds of suppliers, but not to design their cars. No one believes that the articulation of a coherent design philosophy is best handled by a sprawling, leaderless organizational system. Because networks don't have a centralized leadership structure and clear lines of authority, they have real difficulty reaching consensus and setting goals. They can't think strategically; they are chronically prone to conflict and error. How do you make difficult choices about tactics or strategy or philosophical direction when everyone has an equal say?

The Palestine Liberation Organization originated as a network, and the international-relations scholars Mette Eilstrup-Sangiovanni and Calvert Jones argue in a recent essay in *International Security* that this is why it ran into such trouble as it grew: "Structural features typical of networks—the absence of central authority, the unchecked autonomy of rival groups, and the inability to arbitrate quarrels through formal mechanisms—made the P.L.O. excessively vulnerable to outside manipulation and internal strife."

In Germany in the nineteen-seventies, they go on, "the far more unified and successful left-wing terrorists tended to organize hierarchically, with professional management and clear divisions of labor. They were concentrated geographically in universities, where they could establish central leadership, trust, and camaraderie through regular, face-to-face meetings." They seldom betrayed their comrades in arms during police interrogations. Their counterparts on the right were organized as decentralized networks, and had no such discipline. These groups were regularly infiltrated, and members, once arrested, easily gave up their comrades. Similarly, Al Qaeda was most dangerous when it was a unified hierarchy. Now that it has dissipated into a network, it has proved far less effective.

The drawbacks of networks scarcely matter if the network isn't interested in systemic change—if it just wants to frighten or humiliate or make a splash—or if it doesn't need to think strategically. But if you're taking on a powerful and organized establishment you have to be a hierarchy. The Montgomery Bus Boycott required the participation of tens of thousands of people who depended on public transit to get to and from work each day. It lasted a *year*. In order to persuade those people to stay true to the cause, the boycott's organizers tasked each local black church with maintaining morale, and put together a free alternative private carpool service, with forty-eight dispatchers and forty-two pickup stations. Even the White Citizens Council, King later said, conceded that the carpool system moved with "military precision." By the time King came to Birmingham, for the climactic showdown with Police Commissioner Eugene (Bull) Connor, he had a budget of a million dollars, and a hundred full-time staff members on the ground, divided into operational units. The operation itself was divided into steadily escalating phases, mapped out in advance. Support was maintained through consecutive mass meetings rotating from church to church around the city.

Boycotts and sit-ins and nonviolent confrontations—which were the weapons of choice for the civil-rights movement—are high-risk strategies. They leave little room for conflict and error. The moment even one protester deviates from the script and responds to provocation, the moral legitimacy of the entire protest is compromised. Enthusiasts for social media would no doubt have us believe that King's task in Birmingham would have been made infinitely easier had he been able to communicate with his followers through Facebook, and contented himself with tweets from a Birmingham jail. But networks are messy: think of the ceaseless pattern of correction and revision, amendment and debate, that characterizes Wikipedia. If Martin Luther King, Jr., had tried to do a wiki-boycott in Montgomery, he would have been steamrolled by the white power structure. And of what use would a digital communication tool be in a town where ninety-eight per cent of the black community could be reached every Sunday morning at church? The things that King needed in Birmingham—discipline and strategy—were things that online social media cannot provide.

The bible of the social-media movement is Clay Shirky's "Here Comes Everybody." Shirky, who teaches at New York University, sets out to demonstrate the organizing power of the Internet, and he begins with the story of Evan, who worked on Wall Street, and his friend Ivanna, after she left her smart phone, an expensive Sidekick, on the back seat of a New York City taxicab. The telephone company transferred the data on Ivanna's lost phone to a new phone, whereupon she and Evan discovered that the Sidekick was now in the hands of a teen-ager from Queens, who was using it to take photographs of herself and her friends.

When Evan e-mailed the teen-ager, Sasha, asking for the phone back, she replied that his "white ass" didn't deserve to have it back. Miffed, he set up a Web page with her picture and a description of what had happened. He forwarded the link to his friends, and they forwarded it to their friends. Someone found the MySpace page of Sasha's boyfriend, and a link to it found its way onto the site. Someone found her address online and took a video of her home while driving by; Evan posted the video on the site. The story was picked up by the news filter Digg. Evan was now up to ten e-mails a minute. He created a bulletin board for his readers to share their stories, but it crashed under the weight of responses. Evan and Ivanna went to the police, but the police filed the report under "lost," rather than "stolen," which essentially closed the case. "By this point millions of readers were watching," Shirky writes, "and dozens of mainstream news outlets had covered the story." Bowing to the pressure, the N.Y.P.D. reclassified the item as "stolen." Sasha was arrested, and Evan got his friend's Sidekick back.

Shirky's argument is that this is the kind of thing that could never have happened in the pre-Internet age—and he's right. Evan could never have tracked down Sasha. The story of the Sidekick would never have been publicized. An army of people could never have been assembled to wage this fight. The police wouldn't have bowed to the pressure of a lone person who had misplaced something as trivial as a cell phone. The story, to Shirky, illustrates "the ease and speed with which a group can be mobilized for the right kind of cause" in the Internet age.

Shirky considers this model of activism an upgrade. But it is simply a form of organizing which favors the weak-tie connections that give us access to information over the strong-tie connections that help us persevere in the face of danger. It shifts our energies from organizations that

promote strategic and disciplined activity and toward those which promote resilience and adaptability. It makes it easier for activists to express
themselves, and harder for that expression to have any impact. The instruments of social media are well suited to making the existing social order
more efficient. They are not a natural enemy of the status quo. If you are
of the opinion that all the world needs is a little buffing around the edges,
this should not trouble you. But if you think that there are still lunch
counters out there that need integrating it ought to give you pause.

Shirky ends the story of the lost Sidekick by asking, portentously,
"What happens next?"—no doubt imagining future waves of digital protesters. But he has already answered the question. What happens next is
more of the same. A networked, weak-tie world is good at things like helping Wall Streeters get phones back from teen-age girls. *Viva la revolución.*

Why Malcolm Gladwell Should Apologize to Social Media

EDWARD LEE

Malcolm Gladwell is a gifted writer. An author of four best-selling books and many articles for *The New Yorker,* Gladwell likes exposing little recognized phenomena and debunking popular views. His style is more breezy than academic or scientific, yet his anecdotes often sound rather compelling.

One of Gladwell's recent articles, however, may prove to be the tipping point for Gladwell's persuasiveness—and popularity. In an Oct. 4, 2010 article, "Small Change: Why the Revolution Will Not Be Tweeted," Gladwell tried to debunk the popular notion that social media like Facebook, Twitter, and YouTube can be important ingredients to social activism. Gladwell's thesis is that social and political movements need hierarchy to organize and mobilize people, with divisions of labor and, ideally, "strong ties" among people. But, in Gladwell's view, social media like Facebook only establish "weak ties" among people (so-called "friends"), many of whom have never met and who won't risk harm or make real sacrifices for each other.

But didn't social media help spur the political uprisings in Moldova and Iran in 2009? Psshaw, says Gladwell. His evidence? Citing Evgeny Morozov, who is also skeptical of "cyber-utopian" claims that social media will topple totalitarian regimes, Gladwell points out that Moldova had few Twitter accounts identifying Moldova as their location. And, in Iran, a popular hashtag used on Twitter (#iranelection) during the protest was in English, not Farsi, and many tweets were probably from Western countries, not Iran.

These are the only bits of direct evidence Gladwell offers to support his argument. That's it. One doesn't have to be a lawyer to realize Gladwell's proof is lacking.

Indeed, even Gladwell's own source, Morozov, blogged about "Moldova's Twitter Revolution," in which he acknowledged:

"Technology is playing an important role in facilitating these protests. In addition to huge mobilization efforts both on Twitter and Facebook, Moldova's angry youth—especially those who are currently abroad (roughly a quarter of Moldova's population are working abroad due to dire economic conditions back at home)—could follow the events on this livestream provided by a Romanian TV station—directly from the square."

Thus, Gladwell's argument is undermined not only by the fact that location-identification is optional on Twitter, but also by the fact many Moldovans live outside the country. If we credit Morozov's contemporaneous account of the Moldovan uprising, Morozov noted "record-breaking" number of related tweets—most in Romanian, not English—as well as "many" blog posts and "plenty" of YouTube videos and Facebook postings related to the uprising. Morozov himself disavowed Gladwell's type of analysis: "[P]eople who point to the low number of Twitter users in Moldova as proof of the mythical nature of the subject have conceptual difficulties understanding how networks work." Gladwell's discussion of Iran is just as dubious. He ignores the possibility, as one Iranian-American activist reported to the *Washington Post,* that "tweets from a handful of students have been instrumental in getting information to people outside Iran." Even worse, Gladwell ignores perhaps the most important catalyst or galvanizer for the uprising—the shooting death of a young Iranian woman named "Neda" (Neda Agha Soltan) that was captured on video and shared around the world on YouTube to millions of viewers. Without the YouTube video, who knows how many Iranians would have known of her death?

And then there's Egypt. The toppling of the 30-year rule of President Hosni Mubarak last week marked a historic event. By many accounts, a leading catalyst for the uprising was the June 6, 2010 death of Khaled Said, a 28 year-old blogger, who reportedly was beaten to death by Egyptian police—possibly in retaliation for his posting or possession of a video showing police sharing loot from a drug bust. Shortly after Said's death, an anonymous person (now revealed as Wael Ghonim, an Egyptian Google employee in Dubai) created a Facebook page for Khaled Said that showed cellphone photos and YouTube videos of Said, including graphic photos of his beaten corpse. Within weeks, the "We Are All Khaled Said" Facebook page had 130,000 followers. By the beginning of Feb. 2011, it had over 473,000. Today, it has over 773,000 followers, with hundreds of photos and over 60 videos. Although it is impossible to quantify how much Said's death or the Facebook page galvanized the protesters, by the account of one Egyptian protester, "[Khaled Said] is a big part of our revolution." Certainly, the numerous signs with Said's face that protesters held on the streets attest to that fact.

In a Feb. 2, 2011 reply, "Does Egypt Need Twitter?," Gladwell refused to concede the role of social media in the Egyptian protests. "People protested and brought down governments before Facebook was invented," he dismissed. "People with a grievance will always find ways to communicate with each other. How they choose to do it is less interesting, in the end, than why they were driven to do it in the first place." But notice: Gladwell didn't defend his original argument that hierarchy is essential to political movements any longer, much less his central thesis that social media creates only "weak ties" that cannot sustain political revolutions. (Of course, it would be hard to defend Gladwell's positions now in the face of what just happened in Egypt. But facts be damned.) Instead, Gladwell shifted to an entirely different argument that motivations of protesters matter more, in the end, than the modes of communication they choose.

What Gladwell again misses is that the modes of communication, such as social media, may be vital to the success—or failure—of the movement in the first place. Social media can help galvanize and organize people (The "We Are All Khaled Said" Facebook page), while keeping them informed in real time (such as on Twitter). As Ghonim put it in an interview with *60 Minutes,* without social media, the revolution would not have happened. The Facebook page organized and galvanized strangers, and gave them the dates and locations for protests. Hosni Mubarak shut down the Internet in Egypt during the protests in order to make them fail. But that extreme act only fomented the protesters further on the "Friday of Wrath."

Gladwell should consider an important lesson from history: the "ways to communicate with each other" are often a part of what drives people to seek greater political freedoms. If the accounts of Khaled Said's death are accurate, then his death was another example of a government trying to restrict the freedom of the press—here, in the form of a citizen blogger exposing government corruption. An even more extreme restriction was, of course, Egypt's shut down of the Internet there. In the 16th century, the British Crown did the same by restricting most people's access to the printing press, which eventually led to the British people's protests calling for the freedom of the press. That political movement informed the Founding Fathers during the American Revolution and the later adoption of the First Amendment. Then as now, it is mistake to dismiss, as Gladwell does, the "ways to communicate" as "less interesting" when analyzing political movements. Even Mubarak realized that much.

What is most surprising about Gladwell's argument is that it ignores his earlier work in *The Tipping Point: How Little Things Can Make a Big Difference.* In that book, Gladwell theorized that social epidemics are spurred on by a relatively few number of people whom he calls the connectors (with over 100 friends or acquaintances), the mavens (who broker information by word of mouth), and the salesmen (who persuade people by their charisma). Based on the activity of these few actors, a social phenomenon can reach a tipping point and "go viral" drawing in thousands, if not millions more. While Gladwell may not have been writing about political movements, his concepts seem useful in analyzing Egypt. The Facebook page for Khaled Said, along with the photos of him shared through social media, may have been a key connector, maven, and salesman to galvanize the protest. Probably not the only one, but at least an important one. The Facebook page had over 400,000 friends, brokered key information to Egyptians, and provided them with a haunting image of the beaten corpse of Khaled Said, not to mention important dates and locations for upcoming protests, as well as videos of the protests. Under Gladwell's own theory, that would be more than enough to reach a tipping point. *Kolena Khaled Said.*

The Political Power
of Social Media

CLAY SHIRKY

On January 17, 2001, during the impeachment trial of Philippine President Joseph Estrada, loyalists in the Philippine Congress voted to set aside key evidence against him. Less than two hours after the decision was announced, thousands of Filipinos, angry that their corrupt president might be let off the hook, converged on Epifanio de los Santos Avenue, a major crossroads in Manila. The protest was arranged, in part, by forwarded text messages reading, "Go 2 EDSA. Wear blk." The crowd quickly swelled, and in the next few days, over a million people arrived, choking traffic in downtown Manila.

The public's ability to coordinate such a massive and rapid response— close to seven million text messages were sent that week—so alarmed the country's legislators that they reversed course and allowed the evidence to be presented. Estrada's fate was sealed; by January 20, he was gone. The event marked the first time that social media had helped force out a national leader. Estrada himself blamed "the text-messaging generation" for his downfall.

Since the rise of the Internet in the early 1990s, the world's networked population has grown from the low millions to the low billions. Over the same period, social media have become a fact of life for civil society worldwide, involving many actors—regular citizens, activists, nongovernmental organizations, telecommunications firms, software providers, governments. This raises an obvious question for the U.S. government: How does the ubiquity of social media affect U.S. interests, and how should U.S. policy respond to it?

As the communications landscape gets denser, more complex, and more participatory, the networked population is gaining greater access to information, more opportunities to engage in public speech, and an enhanced ability to undertake collective action. In the political arena, as

Shirky, Clay. "The Political Power of Social Media." *Foreign Affairs* 90.1 (Jan./Feb. 2011): n.p. EBSCO. Web. 14 Mar. 2011. © Council on Foreign Relations, Inc.

the protests in Manila demonstrated, these increased freedoms can help loosely coordinated publics demand change.

The Philippine strategy has been adopted many times since. In some cases, the protesters ultimately succeeded, as in Spain in 2004, when demonstrations organized by text messaging led to the quick ouster of Spanish Prime Minister José María Aznar, who had inaccurately blamed the Madrid transit bombings on Basque separatists. The Communist Party lost power in Moldova in 2009 when massive protests coordinated in part by text message, Facebook, and Twitter broke out after an obviously fraudulent election. Around the world, the Catholic Church has faced lawsuits over its harboring of child rapists, a process that started when The Boston Globes 2002 expose of sexual abuse in the church went viral online in a matter of hours.

There are, however, many examples of the activists failing, as in Belarus in March 2006, when street protests (arranged in part by e-mail) against President Aleksandr Lukashenko's alleged vote rigging swelled, then faltered, leaving Lukashenko more determined than ever to control social media. During the June 2009 uprising of the Green Movement in Iran, activists used every possible technological coordinating tool to protest the miscount of votes for Mir Hossein Mousavi but were ultimately brought to heel by a violent crackdown. The Red Shirt uprising in Thailand in 2010 followed a similar but quicker path: protesters savvy with social media occupied downtown Bangkok until the Thai government dispersed the protesters, killing dozens.

The use of social media tools—text messaging, e-mail, photo sharing, social networking, and the like—does not have a single preordained outcome. Therefore, attempts to outline their effects on political action are too often reduced to dueling anecdotes. If you regard the failure of the Belarusian protests to oust Lukashenko as paradigmatic, you will regard the Moldovan experience as an outlier, and vice versa. Empirical work on the subject is also hard to come by, in part because these tools are so new and in part because relevant examples are so rare. The safest characterization of recent quantitative attempts to answer the question, Do digital tools enhance democracy? (such as those by Jacob Groshek and Philip Howard) is that these tools probably do not hurt in the short run and might help in the long run—and that they have the most dramatic effects in states where a public sphere already constrains the actions of the government.

Despite this mixed record, social media have become coordinating tools for nearly all of the world's political movements, just as most of the world's authoritarian governments (and, alarmingly, an increasing number of democratic ones) are trying to limit access to it. In response, the U.S. State Department has committed itself to "Internet freedom" as a specific policy aim. Arguing for the right of people to use the Internet freely is an appropriate policy for the United States, both because it aligns with the strategic goal of strengthening civil society worldwide and because it resonates with American beliefs about freedom of expression. But attempts to yoke the idea of Internet freedom to short-term goals—particularly ones that are country-specific or are intended to help particular dissident groups or encourage regime change—are likely to be ineffective on average. And when they fail, the consequences can be serious.

Although the story of Estrada's ouster and other similar events have led observers to focus on the power of mass protests to topple governments, the potential of social media lies mainly in their support of civil society and the public sphere—change measured in years and decades rather than weeks or months. The U.S. government should maintain Internet freedom as a goal to be pursued in a principled and regime-neutral fashion, not as a tool for effecting immediate policy aims country by country. It should likewise assume that progress will be incremental and, unsurprisingly, slowest in the most authoritarian regimes.

THE PERILS OF INTERNET FREEDOM

In January 2010, U.S. Secretary of State Hillary Clinton outlined how the United States would promote Internet freedom abroad. She emphasized several kinds of freedom, including the freedom to access information (such as the ability to use Wikipedia and Google inside Iran), the freedom of ordinary citizens to produce their own public media (such as the rights of Burmese activists to blog), and the freedom of citizens to converse with one another (such as the Chinese public's capacity to use instant messaging without interference).

Most notably, Clinton announced funding for the development of tools designed to reopen access to the Internet in countries that restrict it. This "instrumental" approach to Internet freedom concentrates on preventing states from censoring outside Web sites, such as Google, YouTube, or that of The New York Times. It focuses only secondarily on public speech by citizens and least of all on private or social uses of digital media. According to this vision, Washington can and should deliver rapid, directed responses to censorship by authoritarian regimes.

The instrumental view is politically appealing, action-oriented, and almost certainly wrong. It overestimates the value of broadcast media while underestimating the value of media that allow citizens to communicate privately among themselves. It overestimates the value of access to information, particularly information hosted in the West, while underestimating the value of tools for local coordination. And it overestimates the importance of computers while underestimating the importance of simpler tools, such as cell phones.

The instrumental approach can also be dangerous. Consider the debacle around the proposed censorship-circumvention software known as Haystack, which, according to its developer, was meant to be a "one-to-one match for how the [Iranian] regime implements censorship." The tool was widely praised in Washington; the U.S. government even granted it an export license. But the program was never carefully vetted, and when security experts examined it, it turned out that it not only failed at its goal of hiding messages from governments but also made it, in the words of one analyst, "possible for an adversary to specifically pinpoint individual users." In contrast, one of the most successful anti-censorship software programs, Freegate, has received little support from the United States, partly because of ordinary bureaucratic delays and partly because the U.S. government is wary of damaging U.S.-Chinese relations: the tool was originally created by Falun Gong, the spiritual movement that the Chinese government has called "an evil cult." The challenges of Freegate and Haystack demonstrate how difficult it is to weaponize social media to pursue country-specific and near-term policy goals.

New media conducive to fostering participation can indeed increase the freedoms Clinton outlined, just as the printing press, the postal service, the telegraph, and the telephone did before. One complaint about the idea of new media as a political force is that most people simply use these tools for commerce, social life, or self-distraction, but this is common to all forms of media. Far more people in the 1500s were reading erotic novels than Martin Luther's "Ninety-five Theses," and far more people before the American Revolution were reading Poor Richard's Almanack than the work of the Committees of Correspondence. But those political works still had an enormous political effect.

Just as Luther adopted the newly practical printing press to protest against the Catholic Church, and the American revolutionaries synchronized their beliefs using the postal service that Benjamin Franklin had designed, today's dissident movements will use any means possible to frame their views and coordinate their actions; it would be impossible to describe the Moldovan Communist Party's loss of Parliament after the 2009 elections without discussing the use of cell phones and online tools by its opponents to mobilize. Authoritarian governments stifle communication among their citizens because they fear, correctly, that a better-coordinated populace would constrain their ability to act without oversight.

Despite this basic truth—that communicative freedom is good for political freedom—the instrumental mode of Internet statecraft is still problematic. It is difficult for outsiders to understand the local conditions of dissent. External support runs the risk of tainting even peaceful opposition as being directed by foreign elements. Dissidents can be exposed by the unintended effects of novel tools. A government's demands for Internet freedom abroad can vary from country to country, depending on the importance of the relationship, leading to cynicism about its motives.

The more promising way to think about social media is as long-term tools that can strengthen civil society and the public sphere. In contrast to the instrumental view of Internet freedom, this can be called the "environmental" view. According to this conception, positive changes in the life of a country, including pro-democratic regime change, follow, rather than precede, the development of a strong public sphere. This is not to say that popular movements will not successfully use these tools to discipline or even oust their governments, but rather that U.S. attempts to direct such uses are likely to do more harm than good. Considered in this light, Internet freedom is a long game, to be conceived of and supported not as a separate agenda but merely as an important input to the more fundamental political freedoms.

THE THEATER OF COLLAPSE

Any discussion of political action in repressive regimes must take into account the astonishing fall of communism in 1989 in eastern Europe and the subsequent collapse of the Soviet Union in 1991. Throughout the Cold War, the United States invested in a variety of communications tools, including broadcasting the Voice of America radio station, hosting an American pavilion in Moscow (home of the famous Nixon-Khrushchev "kitchen debate"), and smuggling Xerox machines behind the Iron Curtain to aid the underground press, or samizdat. Yet despite this emphasis on communications, the end of the Cold War was triggered not by a defiant uprising of Voice of America listeners but by economic change. As the price of oil fell while that of wheat spiked, the Soviet model of selling expensive oil to buy cheap wheat stopped working. As a result, the Kremlin was forced to secure loans from the West, loans that would have been put at risk had the government intervened militarily in the affairs of non-Russian states. In 1989, one could argue, the ability of citizens to communicate, considered against the background of macro-economic forces, was largely irrelevant.

But why, then, did the states behind the Iron Curtain not just let their people starve? After all, the old saying that every country is three meals away from revolution turned out to be sadly incorrect in the twentieth century; it is possible for leaders to survive even when millions die. Stalin did it in the 1930s, Mao did it in the 1960s, and Kim Jong Il has done it more than once in the last two decades. But the difference between those cases and the 1989 revolutions was that the leaders of East Germany, Czechoslovakia, and the rest faced civil societies strong enough to resist. The weekly demonstrations in East Germany, the Charter 77 civic movement in Czechoslovakia, and the Solidarity movement in Poland all provided visible governments in waiting.

The ability of these groups to create and disseminate literature and political documents, even with simple photocopiers, provided a visible alternative to the communist regimes. For large groups of citizens in these countries, the political and, even more important, economic bankruptcy of the government was no longer an open secret but a public fact. This made it difficult and then impossible for the regimes to order their troops to take on such large groups.

Thus, it was a shift in the balance of power between the state and civil society that led to the largely peaceful collapse of communist control. The state's ability to use violence had been weakened, and the civil society that would have borne the brunt of its violence had grown stronger. When civil society triumphed, many of the people who had articulated opposition to the communist regimes—such as Tadeusz Mazowiecki in Poland and Vaclav Havel in Czechoslovakia—became the new political leaders of those countries. Communications tools during the Cold War did not cause governments to collapse, but they helped the people take power from the state when it was weak.

The idea that media, from the Voice of America to samizdat, play a supporting role in social change by strengthening the public sphere echoes the historical role of the printing press. As the German philosopher Jürgen Habermas argued in his 1962 book, *The Structural Transformation of the Public Sphere,* the printing press helped democratize Europe by providing space for discussion and agreement among politically engaged citizens, often before the state had fully democratized, an argument extended by later scholars, such as Asa Briggs, Elizabeth Eisenstein, and Paul Starr.

Political freedom has to be accompanied by a civil society literate enough and densely connected enough to discuss the issues presented to the public. In a famous study of political opinion after the 1948 U.S. presidential election, the sociologists Elihu Katz and Paul Lazarsfeld discovered that mass media alone do not change people's minds; instead, there is a two-step process. Opinions are first transmitted by the media, and then they get echoed by friends, family members, and colleagues. It is in this second, social step that political opinions are formed. This is the step in which the Internet in general, and social media in particular, can make a difference. As with the printing press, the Internet spreads not just media consumption but media production as well—it allows people to privately and publicly articulate and debate a welter of conflicting views.

A slowly developing public sphere, where public opinion relies on both media and conversation, is the core of the environmental view of Internet freedom. As opposed to the self-aggrandizing view that the West holds the source code for democracy—and if it were only made accessible, the remaining autocratic states would crumble—the environmental view assumes that little political change happens without the dissemination and adoption of ideas and opinions in the public sphere. Access to information is far less important, politically, than access to conversation. Moreover, a public sphere is more likely to emerge in a society as a result of people's dissatisfaction with matters of economics or day-to-day governance than from their embrace of abstract political ideals.

To take a contemporary example, the Chinese government today is in more danger of being forced to adopt democratic norms by middle-class members of the ethnic Han majority demanding less corrupt local governments than it is by Uighurs or Tibetans demanding autonomy. Similarly, the One Million Signatures Campaign, an Iranian women's rights movement that focuses on the repeal of laws inimical to women, has been more successful in liberalizing the behavior of the Iranian government than the more confrontational Green Movement.

For optimistic observers of public demonstrations, this is weak tea, but both the empirical and the theoretical work suggest that protests, when effective, are the end of a long process, rather than a replacement for it. Any real commitment by the United States to improving political freedom worldwide should concentrate on that process—which can only occur when there is a strong public sphere.

THE CONSERVATIVE DILEMMA

Disciplined and coordinated groups, whether businesses or governments, have always had an advantage over undisciplined ones: they have an easier time engaging in collective action because they have an orderly way of directing the action of their members. Social media can compensate for the disadvantages of undisciplined groups by reducing the costs of coordination. The anti-Estrada movement in the Philippines used the ease of sending and forwarding text messages to organize a massive group with no need (and no time) for standard managerial control. As a result, larger, looser groups can now take on some kinds of coordinated action, such as protest movements and public media campaigns, that were previously reserved for formal organizations. For political movements, one of the main forms of coordination is what the military calls "shared awareness," the ability of each member of a group to not only understand the situation at hand but also understand that everyone else does, too. Social media increase shared awareness by propagating messages through social networks. The anti-Aznar protests in Spain gained momentum so quickly precisely because the millions of people spreading the message were not part of a hierarchical organization.

The Chinese anticorruption protests that broke out in the aftermath of the devastating May 2008 earthquake in Sichuan are another example of such ad hoc synchronization. The protesters were parents, particularly mothers, who had lost their only children in the collapse of shoddily built schools, the result of collusion between construction firms and the local government. Before the earthquake, corruption in the country's construction industry was an open secret. But when the schools collapsed, citizens began sharing documentation of the damage and of their protests through social media tools. The consequences of government corruption were made broadly visible, and it went from being an open secret to a public truth.

The Chinese government originally allowed reporting on the post-earthquake protests, but abruptly reversed itself in June. Security forces began arresting protesters and threatening journalists when it became clear that the protesters were demanding real local reform and not merely state reparations. From the government's perspective, the threat was not that citizens were aware of the corruption, which the state could do nothing about in the short run. Beijing was afraid of the possible effects if this awareness became shared: it would have to either enact reforms or respond in a way that would alarm more citizens. After all, the prevalence of camera phones has made it harder to carry out a widespread but undocumented crackdown.

This condition of shared awareness—which is increasingly evident in all modern states—creates what is commonly called "the dictator's dilemma" but that might more accurately be described by the phrase coined by the media theorist Briggs: "the conservative dilemma," so named because it applies not only to autocrats but also to democratic governments and to religious and business leaders. The dilemma is created by new media that increase public access to speech or assembly, with the spread of such media, whether photocopiers or Web browsers, a state accustomed to having a monopoly on public speech finds itself called to account for anomalies between its view of events and the public's. The two responses to the conservative dilemma are censorship and propaganda. But neither of these is as effective a source of control as the enforced silence of the citizens. The state will censor critics or produce propaganda as it needs to, but both of those actions have higher costs than simply not having any critics to silence or reply to in the first place. But if a government were to shut down Internet access or ban cell phones, it would risk radicalizing otherwise pro-regime citizens or harming the economy.

The conservative dilemma exists in part because political speech and apolitical speech are not mutually exclusive. Many of the South Korean teenage girls who turned out in Seoul's Cheonggyecheon Park in 2008 to protest U.S. beef imports were radicalized in the discussion section of a web site dedicated to Dong Bang Shin Ki, a South Korean boy band. DBSK is not a political group, and the protesters were not typical political actors. But that online community, with around 800,000 active members, amplified the second step of Katz and Lazarsfeld's two-step process by allowing members to form political opinions through conversation.

Popular culture also heightens the conservative dilemma by providing cover for more political uses of social media. Tools specifically designed for dissident use are politically easy for the state to shut down, whereas tools in broad use become much harder to censor without risking politicizing the larger group of otherwise apolitical actors. Ethan Zuckerman of Harvard's Berkman Center for Internet and Society calls this "the cute cat theory of digital activism." Specific tools designed to defeat state censorship (such as proxy servers) can be shut down with little political penalty, but broader tools that the larger population uses to, say, share pictures of cute cats are harder to shut down.

For these reasons, it makes more sense to invest in social media as general, rather than specifically political, tools to promote self-governance. The norm of free speech is inherently political and far from universally shared. To the degree that the United States makes free speech a first-order goal, it should expect that goal to work relatively well in democratic countries that are allies, less well in undemocratic countries that are allies, and least of all in undemocratic countries that are not allies. But nearly every country in the world desires economic growth. Since governments jeopardize that growth when they ban technologies that can be used for both political and economic coordination, the United States should rely on countries' economic incentives to allow widespread media use. In other words, the U.S. government should work for conditions that increase the conservative dilemma, appealing to states' self-interest rather than the contentious virtue of freedom, as a way to create or strengthen countries' public spheres.

SOCIAL MEDIA SKEPTICISM

There are, broadly speaking, two arguments against the idea that social media will make a difference in national politics. The first is that the tools are themselves ineffective, and the second is that they produce as much harm to democratization as good, because repressive governments are becoming better at using these tools to suppress dissent.

The critique of ineffectiveness, most recently offered by Malcolm Gladwell in The New Yorker, concentrates on examples of what has been termed "slacktivism," whereby casual participants seek social change through low-cost activities, such as joining Facebook's "Save Darfur" group, that are long on bumper-sticker sentiment and short on any useful action. The critique is correct but not central to the question of social media's power; the fact that barely committed actors cannot click their way to a better world does not mean that committed actors cannot use social media effectively. Recent protest movements—including a movement against fundamentalist vigilantes in India in 2009, the beef protests in South Korea in 2008, and protests against education laws in Chile in 2006—have used social media not as a replacement for real-world action but as a way to coordinate it. As a result, all of those protests exposed participants to the threat of violence, and in some cases its actual use. In fact, the adoption of these tools (especially cell phones) as a way to coordinate and document real-world action is so ubiquitous that it will probably be a part of all future political movements.

This obviously does not mean that every political movement that uses these tools will succeed, because the state has not lost the power to react. This points to the second, and much more serious, critique of social media as tools for political improvement—namely, that the state is gaining increasingly sophisticated means of monitoring, interdicting, or co-opting these tools. The use of social media, the scholars Rebecca MacKinnon of the New America Foundation and Evgeny Morozov of the Open Society Institute have argued, is just as likely to strengthen authoritarian regimes as it is to weaken them. The Chinese government has spent considerable effort perfecting several systems for controlling political threats from social media. The least important of these is its censorship and surveillance program. Increasingly, the government recognizes that threats to its legitimacy are coming from inside the state and that blocking the Web site of The New York Times does little to prevent grieving mothers from airing their complaints about corruption.

The Chinese system has evolved from a relatively simple filter of incoming Internet traffic in the mid-1990s to a sophisticated operation that not only limits outside information but also uses arguments about nationalism and public morals to encourage operators of Chinese Web services to censor their users and users to censor themselves. Because its goal is to prevent information from having politically synchronizing effects, the state does not need to censor the Internet comprehensively; rather, it just needs to minimize access to information.

Authoritarian states are increasingly shutting down their communications grids to deny dissidents the ability to coordinate in real time and broadcast documentation of an event. This strategy also activates the conservative dilemma, creating a short-term risk of alerting the population at large to political conflict. When the government of Bahrain banned Google Earth after an annotated map of the royal family's annexation of public land began circulating, the effect was to alert far more Bahrainis to the offending map than knew about it originally. So widely did the news spread that the government relented and reopened access after four days.

Such shutdowns become more problematic for governments if they are long-lived. When antigovernment protesters occupied Bangkok in the summer of 2010, their physical presence disrupted Bangkok's shopping district, but the state's reaction, cutting off significant parts of the Thai telecommunications infrastructure, affected people far from the capital.

The approach creates an additional dilemma for the state—there can be no modern economy without working phones—and so its ability to shut down communications over large areas or long periods is constrained.

In the most extreme cases, the use of social media tools is a matter of life and death, as with the proposed death sentence for the blogger Hossein Derakhshan in Iran (since commuted to 19 and a half years in prison) or the suspicious hanging death of Oleg Bebenin, the founder of the Belarusian opposition Web site Charter 97. Indeed, the best practical reason to think that social media can help bring political change is that both dissidents and governments think they can. All over the world, activists believe in the utility of these tools and take steps to use them accordingly. And the governments they contend with think social media tools are powerful, too, and are willing to harass, arrest, exile, or kill users in response. One way the United States can heighten the conservative dilemma without running afoul of as many political complications is to demand the release of citizens imprisoned for using media in these ways. Anything that constrains the worst threats of violence by the state against citizens using these tools also increases the conservative dilemma.

LOOKING AT THE LONG RUN

To the degree that the United States pursues Internet freedom as a tool of statecraft, it should de-emphasize anti-censorship tools, particularly those aimed at specific regimes, and increase its support for local public speech and assembly more generally. Access to information is not unimportant, of course, but it is not the primary way social media constrain autocratic rulers or benefit citizens of a democracy. Direct, U.S. government—sponsored support for specific tools or campaigns targeted at specific regimes risk creating backlash that a more patient and global application of principles will not.

This entails reordering the State Departments Internet freedom goals. Securing the freedom of personal and social communication among a state's population should be the highest priority, closely followed by securing individual citizens' ability to speak in public. This reordering would reflect the reality that it is a strong civil society—one in which citizens have freedom of assembly—rather than access to Google or YouTube, that does the most to force governments to serve their citizens.

As a practical example of this, the United States should be at least as worried about Egypt's recent controls on the mandatory licensing of group-oriented text-messaging services as it is about Egypt's attempts to add new restrictions on press freedom. The freedom of assembly that such text-messaging services support is as central to American democratic ideals as is freedom of the press. Similarly, South Korea's requirement that citizens register with their real names for certain Internet services is an attempt to reduce their ability to surprise the state with the kind of coordinated action that took place during the 2008 protest in Seoul. If the United States does not complain as directly about this policy as it does about Chinese censorship, it risks compromising its ability to argue for Internet freedom as a global ideal.

More difficult, but also essential, will be for the U.S. government to articulate a policy of engagement with the private companies and organizations that host the networked public sphere. Services based in the United States, such as Facebook, Twitter, Wikipedia, and YouTube, and those based overseas, such as QQ. (a Chinese instant-messaging service), WikiLeaks (a repository of leaked documents whose servers are in Sweden), Tuenti (a Spanish social network), and Naver (a Korean one), are among the sites used most for political speech, conversation, and coordination. And the world's wireless carriers transmit text messages, photos, and videos from cell phones through those sites. How much can these entities be expected to support freedom of speech and assembly for their users?

The issue here is analogous to the questions about freedom of speech in the United States in private but commercial environments, such as those regarding what kind of protests can be conducted in shopping malls. For good or ill, the platforms supporting the networked public sphere are privately held and run; Clinton committed the United States to working with those companies, but it is unlikely that without some legal framework, as exists for real-world speech and action, moral suasion will be enough to convince commercial actors to support freedom of speech and assembly.

It would be nice to have a flexible set of short-term digital tactics that could be used against different regimes at different times. But the requirements of real-world statecraft mean that what is desirable may not be likely. Activists in both repressive and democratic regimes will use the Internet and related tools to try to effect change in their countries, but Washington's ability to shape or target these changes is limited. Instead, Washington should adopt a more general approach, promoting freedom of speech, freedom of the press, and freedom of assembly everywhere. And it should understand that progress will be slow. Only by switching from an instrumental to an environmental view of the effects of social media on the public sphere will the United States be able to take advantage of the long-term benefits these tools promise—even though that may mean accepting short-term disappointment.

Why 'Slacktivism' Matters

SHANNON FISHER

We all have at least one social or political issue that gets our blood boiling. The question is whether it boils vigorously enough to incite action.

Of course, the majority of us vent our frustrations about these issues at the water cooler and on social media, rather than marching in the streets. We create an echo chamber of like-minded people with whom we can openly share opinions and commiserate grievances. But when the discussion expands beyond the insulation of that echo chamber, true dialogue begins.

In April of 2014, hundreds of girls in Nigeria were kidnapped from their school by the militant group, Boko Haram. Of those taken, 223 are still missing. If we want to facilitate their return, the solution is simple! All we need to do is compose a post on social media condemning the horrific actions and include the appropriate hashtag in the post—#Bring-BackOurGirls, in this case—and we're done. A significant contribution toward solving the problem has been made. Hasn't it?

While the idea that a single post on social media could have an iota of impact on a global issue might sound absurd, it can actually be the catalyst for a successful awareness campaign given the right set of circumstances. A sizable, active social media network can propel that one post into a trajectory that effectively reaches millions. We cannot discount the enormous potential of a well-intended 140-character post in raising awareness, though common sense and experience clearly indicate that significant additional effort—both online and offline—is required to reach genuine solutions and resolutions.

SLACKTIVISM VS. ACTIVISM

There are two types of online activists: people whose efforts end with clicking the "share" button, and those who are willing to take further steps to delve deeply into a cause. The former is what is pejoratively known as a slacktivist, defined as a person who believes he or she is enacting real change in the world with a few simple clicks of a mouse. While slacktivists are often maligned, they do play an integral role in raising awareness. A truly powerful agent for change, though, makes a strong commitment to act in whatever manner necessary to achieve the desired result. Much can be accomplished via online activism beyond the simple sharing of posts, and it is usually necessary to pursue even further action offline. Once groups are organized and strategies are developed online, which is the crux of social media activism, we mobilize in person. This is when we really get things done.

HOW IT WORKS

It all starts with one post—one post that usually includes information about a topic, sometimes linking to an article with facts and figures, and a hashtag related to the post. Friends and followers who see this post and agree with the sentiment will like/favorite and share/re-tweet the original post, garnering it exponentially more exposure as each person in the network disseminates the information within their own network. If enough people include the hashtag, the hashtag will start trending (i.e., listed as one of the most discussed topics at that moment). People who might not normally have been exposed to the original post will jump on the trend bandwagon, creating a boom of awareness. It is through viral activity like this that hundreds of thousands of people know to show up to a march at a specific date and time. The above trajectory is, of course, assuming you have a strong and active following on social media. The #BringBackOurGirls campaign was joined by hundreds of celebrities and political figures, along with their millions of followers, in an attempt to put public pressure on the Nigerian government to find the girls, or on Boko Haram to release them. Sadly, no tangible action came from the campaign, but it drew significant attention worldwide. Should something like this kidnapping happen again, the international spotlight will ensure that appropriate attention is paid to the issue.

TOOLS FOR ONLINE ORGANIZING

Long-since proven methods of activism—letter-writing and phone campaigns, marches, petitions, sit-ins, visits to legislators, knocking on doors—are still the most effective to enact change, but now we have some help from the Internet to make them much more efficient.

Facebook, Twitter, Instagram, Google+, Blog Talk Radio, YouTube, and Pastebin are all vehicles to instantaneously share information across a scattered network. We can use these forums to communicate internally with group members, or to share information directly with the public. For a more personal connection, programs like Skype enable interactive video conferencing. There is no single model for online activism.

I see Facebook as the most effective venue because it offers every tool needed to organize. Users can create groups, which are essentially private chat rooms where like-minded people can brainstorm, plan events, or simply discuss the issues. When the time comes to move on from cyberspace, the group's roster is a ready-made list of potential volunteers.

Event pages enable you to schedule a rally, invite your friends and colleagues, and ask them to invite all of their friends. This will normally yield a nice crowd at an event. Events can also be virtual. An example of a virtual event would be a "Twitter bomb," during which hundreds of people tweet simultaneously, using the same hashtags and targeting legislators. The point is to get a topic trending and flood the feeds of lawmakers with awareness of the issue. As implausible as it sounds, I witnessed a Congressman change his vote on a piece of legislation due to a Twitter bomb.

TO THE STREETS AND STATEHOUSES

Most online activists are volunteers, fueled by passion for the cause but lacking the resources to mobilize in person to protest or lobby legislators. Permitting, equipment, and sometimes lodging for events are expensive. These groups all need help, specifically time and money. You might be surprised by what can be done on social media in just an hour or two per week.

Enacting real change on the issues that get our blood boiling requires making an effort. But, activism is activism.

Slacktivism:
The Downfall of Millennials

CHARLOTTE ROBERTSON

Information is at our fingertips. Thousands of articles circulate the web each day, making knowledge about the surrounding world more accessible to us than it has ever been before.

For the past few decades, we have been made increasingly aware of all that the world encompasses—whether it is culture, natural occurrences, politics, or atrocity. This accessibility has largely been dictated by the emergence of new technology and media, allowing major historical events to be globally communicated via real-time news by primary sources.

This phenomena is often referred to as globalization, a buzzword that has become increasingly popular since the 1990's, as society tries to decide what this interconnected, overlapping system of shared experiences means in the context of our own lives.

In many ways, there is beauty to globalization. Globalization lets us connect to one another in ways unimaginable a century ago. It allows us to speak face to face despite distance via programs like Skype; it allows us to view a constant stream of photos and events, seeing our friends lives on a daily basis; it allows us to send a quick message in a matter of seconds via text; and it allows us to voice our opinions on a global platform, reaching cross cultural audiences.

But as we connect, do we also disconnect? As we figure out ways to feel closer, we must question if it is an artificial feeling. For how connected can we be if we are behind a screen?

Being behind a computer screen has become a more comfortable form of interaction for most of our generation, rather than interpersonal communication. It allows us to voice our opinions without fear of rejection and to project our social viewpoints without much thought.

These two aspects of social media are single handedly killing histori-

Robertson, Charlotte. "Slacktivism: The Downfall of Millennials." *Huffington Post.* 14 Oct. 2014. <http://www.huffingtonpost.com/charlotte-robertson/slacktivism-the-downfall-_b_5984336.html>. © Charlotte Robertson.

— 129 —

cal forms of activism—marching, public speaking, protests, physical petitions, and strikes. Social media outlets like Facebook and Twitter have allowed us to share a message that we find important, and then step away from it, as we continue to scan our friends' feeds.

We continuously absorb social justice messages, but we don't take the time to act upon them. This inaction is commonly referred to as "slacktivism" or "hashtag activism." And we have all taken part in it. There have been a slew of examples in the past year.

#BringBackOurGirls began to encourage political leaders both in the US and Nigeria to put resources into finding the 300 schoolgirls who were kidnapped by the Boko Haram, an Islamist militant group. Though the movement gained support from civilians across the globe through the support of celebrities, and even the First Lady, Michelle Obama, it was largely forgotten within a few weeks. However, the mothers, fathers, siblings, and friends of the Chibok girls have surely not forgotten them. What did our momentary, fleeting compassion mean to them?

The ALS Ice Bucket Challenge is another example of a largely internet-based social awareness campaign. Despite the campaigns widespread success, the challenge has done little to educate the public on ALS or the importance of donations. Many participants in the challenge completed it for shock-value and neither researched the debilitating disease or donated a dollar. The average participant spent more money on the ice than on funding research that could help make the lives of ALS patients better. What do the thousands of Ice Bucket Challenge videos really mean to ALS patients?

The most recent prevalently broadcasted social injustice took place in Ferguson, Missouri when Michael Brown, an unarmed, black teenager, was shot and killed by a police officer. How quickly will we forget this? What atrocity will come next to divert our attention? How can we create social change when we refuse to devote time and thought to our actions? Who is really listening to us when the only voice we are projecting is stuck inside a computer?

Social media outlets have been beneficial in creating a platform for marginalized groups to communicate and share experiences. After Michael Brown was killed, the hashtag "#IfTheyGunnedMeDown" began trending on Twitter. Members of the movement posted a photo that they thought truly depicted themselves, as well as an image that they thought a media outlet would use if they were killed. The first photo showed them in good light, in a graduation cap, with their children, or in military attire.

The second photo portrayed them as a stereotype, as a thug, certainly not an upstanding citizen. These photos helped show how Michael Brown's death was framed, as a person of color, by the media.

Twitter has also proved a helpful forum for activists to start conversations on a large scale. Suey Park, an Asian-American activist, used the twitter hashtag "#NotYourAsianSidekick" to begin a forum for women of color rejecting American society's normative stereotyping of Asian women. With this, Park was interested in creating a tool to develop conversation and encourage decolonization.

Social media can be used as a forum to promote ideology and begin conversation. However, it is unacceptable to not move past the point of conversation, into action. It is unacceptable to not continue to seek information, to ask questions, and to demand answers.

When we "retweet," when we "hashtag," when we "share," we allow ourselves to feel more moral. We feel like we are good people because we have shown a level of awareness. But don't we, in fact, become guiltier of perpetuating social injustice once aware? Our inaction upon awareness makes us implicit in a form of systematic oppression. In truth, our new form of activism, our "slacktivism" enables us to be lazy, cowardly, and, in return, to feel good about it.

As a communications major, I find this deeply troubling. I question what the importance of my profession will be in a decade. I wanted to enter the field so that I could empower people to be agents of change. But when I see how media is overwhelmingly used by our generation, often by myself, I wonder what my impact will realistically be. What is the point of my skill set when people will only forward information on to the next person, rather than receiving it as a call to action, and acting upon it?

Activism should not be an isolating experience. Activism should be rallying, speeches, emotion. So let's step away from the computer, put down the cell phone, and reconnect with the real world in order to take on and help solve its problems.

Relationships

Don't Dismiss Online Relationships as Fantasy

REGINA LYNN

Last month, three unrelated stories challenged the idea that internet relationships are just fantasy and therefore less important, less powerful and less real than offline relationships.

They aren't.

First, I read the *Wired* magazine piece about Thomas Montgomery, a married father of two in New York state. Montgomery invented two alternate identities and got both of them involved online with the 17-year-old girl persona of Mary, a forty-something married woman in West Virginia, whom he met at the games site, Pogo.com. He then became so jealous that she was also seeing his co-worker online, that he shot the guy dead in the parking lot after work.

In real life. Where you can't just get a snack, go pee and log back in.

This is "just fantasy"? No. At least, it's no more fantastic than any other murderer's fantasy image of himself as a tough guy out to keep other men off his woman. Montgomery's was a real—albeit twisted—relationship, based on power and manipulation rather than love or sex, and one that resulted in real tragedy.

A *Wall Street Journal* article described a couple who met online three years ago and whose offline marriage is now on the rocks because of the husband's immersion in Second Life. Or maybe he initially immersed himself in Second Life because the marriage wasn't going so well; it's hard to tell.

Either way, his dedicated online involvement includes owning several businesses, adopting two dogs and getting married. He downplays his in-world marriage as "part of the game," a fantasy he and his Second Life partner have no intention of pursuing offline.

Yet I find it unlikely that a person would devote the majority of his working hours to something that is simply "a game."

Virtual worlds are boring when there's no one to play with; you don't go in there just to defy gravity and buy new costumes for your dolls. You're there for the people—and you don't spend all day every day with mere casual acquaintances, either. Only relationships with real emotional attachment could foster such commitment.

Last week the *Houston Chronicle* reported that one in three women who met partners through online dating sites had sex with them "on the first date"—and that 75 percent of those women didn't use condoms.

The study contrasts this apparently risky behavior with the extensive care women take to stay safe in other ways, like doing formal background checks, meeting in a public place, telling a friend whom they're meeting, and setting up check-in calls.

In this story, an MIT professor of behavioral economics is quoted as saying, "When somebody's sitting by their laptop at home and writing these sterile e-mails to each other, there's no sense of emotionality.... But when they meet and they get aroused, life changes."

Believe me, professor. If the e-mails were sterile or lacking in emotionality, the men would never get to the "first date" stage, much less sex.

Those pre-date e-mails and chats and dancing in virtual clubs build a relationship quickly. A real relationship. Sometimes, it's a relationship so hot that if you climax en route to the "first date," you don't consider it premature.

The common thread among these stories is that people get deeply involved in online relationships and make decisions about their real lives. Calling any of these online relationships "fantasy" dismisses the impact they have on the people involved and on those closest to them.

We all know we do things in the heat of the moment that we might not if we stepped back and thought about it for a while. Online environments can extend that "heat of the moment" feeling over long periods of time; physical environments often don't. And then we do stupid things, like completely ignore our other relationships to be with our online lovers, instead of staying in balance. Or we get caught having IM sex at work and get fired.

Very rarely does someone lose it as completely as Montgomery did. And yet, sexual jealousy is not a new motive for murder. This one is news because of the twists that can only happen online: Two baby boomers successfully fooled each other into believing they were barely legal. But the bonds that formed, however unhealthy, turned out to be all too real.

Even people who might point to the Montgomery case as an example of why the internet should be turned off forever know it's an extreme example. Meanwhile, the rest of us can say, "That's absurd, that doesn't apply to me at all," and still rush blindly into troubles of our own.

For all that I have broadened my horizons since the first Sex Drive column more than four years ago, I have yet to encounter anything that challenges my core belief: Relationships are real wherever they form.

That's why we're so desperate to pretend it's all fantasy if it's online, so we can make the hard, painful, life-crushing parts go away. And that's why I get my panties in a bunch when people try to dismiss the reality of sex in virtual spaces. I'm all for cybersex, of course, but let's not pretend it doesn't have real consequences.

Sex educator Cory Silverberg notes on his blog that "maybe we want to pretend that what happens online stays online because so often, we want it to."

But anyone who has been affected by online love knows the emotions don't turn on when we log on and turn off when we log off.

I mean, just look at Jazz Asylum and Chelle Moore, also known as Joe Trykoski and Michelle Pignatano. They met in Second Life last October and got married in-world. This spring, Michelle moved across four states into Joe's apartment, and they continued to play together in Second Life.

Last month in Chicago, Joe stopped the music at the Second Life Community Convention Masquerade Ball (which felt a lot like being in-world with the props, music and costumes), dropped to one knee, and proposed to Michelle. No one doubted the emotion in her voice when she said yes. The crowd cheered, and the dancing continued.

Now tell me it's just fantasy.

See you next time,

Regina Lynn

Rude People, Not Tech, Cause Bad Manners

REGINA LYNN

I don't remember my university offering courses on how to make friends. It might have—but I didn't know about it, and neither did any of my friends. No one ever mentioned hearing of such a thing.

Yet New York University now offers a seminar called Facebook in the Flesh, reports the *New Yorker*. The idea is to help freshmen who already know dozens of their classmates online but who worry they don't know how to make new friends in person. That's the fear and the whimsy behind NYU assistant dean David Schachter's decision to hold the workshop, even though he says he's never been on Facebook and his advice to students parallels exactly what users already do online.

The mind boggles.

It makes me think of the moaning and wailing surrounding mobile devices and how we supposedly don't connect "for real" anymore. How we're allegedly replacing real relationships with fake ones, true intimacy with illusion and strong social bonding with pseudo-social networking.

This is all because a lot of people apparently spend a lot of time conversing online rather than in the flesh. And in order to keep up with all these relationships, we're supposedly not being as attentive to the people around us as we should. Not our loved ones, mind you, but the people we encounter casually as we go about our lives: bank tellers, dog walkers, grocers.

Tell me again why I should spend less time with the people I love and more time with strangers?

Convince me that it's more important to yak with a stranger at the neighborhood coffee house than it is to text conversation with my dear friend Monique. It might look like I'm ignoring a passing acquaintance in order to "use my phone." But actually I'm checking in with a new mom

Lynn, Regina. "Rude People, Not Tech, Cause Bad Manners." *Wired* 21 Sept. 2007. Web. 12 Mar. 2011. <http://www.wired.com/culture/lifestyle/commentary/sexdrive/2007/09/sexdrive_0921>. © Conde Nast Publications, Inc.

who is running home, baby and business on her own while her partner's job has him commuting to Canada temporarily. (Hooray for unlimited international minutes!)

Explain to me why I am contributing to The Decline of Morals and Manners in This Society because I prefer to attend to friends and lovers through our cell phones rather than allow geography to determine who I can and can't relate with.

I don't dismiss out of hand the concerns about techno-communication. Daniel Goleman, a proponent of the science of empathy, intuition and emotion and a thinker I trust, writes about a mass wave of disconnection in the introduction to his book *Social Intelligence.*

In explaining how mood and emotion are contagious, he notes the ripple effect of rude behavior and how spreading negativity and hurt feelings damages the human web more than most people realize.

But rudeness is a separate issue from connectivity. Mobile devices should not make us impolite.

I recently caught myself flirting by text message while checking into a hotel. I didn't particularly want to connect with the hotel guy—I wanted to keep going with the sweet (and spicy) nothings.

It was an almost physical wrench to set the phone down even for five minutes. Yet to do otherwise would be as churlish as carrying on a conversation with a companion as if the clerk wasn't even there. (Which does happen, alas, but not by me.)

We all need to accept responsibility for our manners.

But harnessing technology to nurture our existing relationships has not damaged our ability to connect "for real." Connectivity gives shy swains time to craft what they want to say, and it gives extroverts layers of interaction to satisfy their craving for people contact and shared energy.

People once took for granted the idea that meeting new people was easier for some folks than others. And I think people who are not comfortable using technology to do that, who simply can't do it, or who have burned out or become overwhelmed by technology worry about those who can handle it.

I think they feel left out. Like we're in a secret club they can't get into, or didn't enjoy once they got through the door.

Mobile service providers know exactly what we use cell phones for. Cingular's commercials about what dropped calls can do to lovers get right to the heart of the matter. And Vodaphone has a great one about a sleeping model, an opportunist and the trouble we can get into with camera phones.

Just like the fears people express about internet users "replacing" love and sex with delusion and cybersex, the concerns about "everyone" interacting through devices rather than in person miss the point. Two points.

For one thing, many of the people we're interacting with through our mobiles are our intimates. They are people we feel so connected with, we want to be with them across time and distance.

For another, we have to trust each other to disconnect when we need to. I'm not going to bemoan a "dependence" on technology-facilitated communication (as if our entire economy isn't based on such a thing!) when we can all put down the phone or walk away from the computer when we get overwhelmed. We are not going to wreck society simply because we can choose who we want to talk to at any given time, based not on proximity but on attachment and affection.

I even believe we are strengthening human bonds through these technologically supported connections.

With mobile devices especially, we're sharing the love. Our mobiles are less anonymous and more personal than online message boards or blog comments, and we use them as extensions of ourselves and our relationships. They define "personal tech." And the very limitation that makes flirting and lovemaking so fun also makes it too frustrating to bother with flaming and hate speech.

I have also found that nurturing relationships through tech has taught me to be more forgiving and patient. I'm a better listener, because texting forces me to slow down. I've also become better about asking for clarification when I don't understand something, rather than jumping to a conclusion; I don't agonize over the question, "What did he mean by that?"

Modern relationships—whether between colleagues, friends or lovers—flow between flesh and technology more easily every day.

Let's accept that we've been dazzled by the novelty of our devices long enough and dust off our manners. Then let's embrace the truth that emotions are contagious, and ensure that the emotions we inspire in even the most casual of encounters are pleasant or at least neutral.

And then let's get back on our devices and send a text message so hot, so loving, so clever that our bosom buddy cannot help but pass that warmth on to someone else.

See you in a fortnight,
Regina Lynn

You Have No Friends

FARHAD MANJOO

At 1:37 a.m. on Jan. 8, Mark Zuckerberg, the 24-year-old founder and CEO of Facebook, posted a message on the company's blog with news of a milestone: The site had just added its 150-millionth member. Facebook now has users on every continent, with half of them logging in at least once a day. "If Facebook were a country, it would be the eighth most populated in the world, just ahead of Japan, Russia and Nigeria," Zuckerberg wrote. This People's Republic of Facebook would also have a terrible population-growth problem. Like most communications networks, Facebook obeys classic network-effects laws: It gets better—more useful, more entertaining—as more people join it, which causes it to grow even faster still. It was just last August that Facebook hit 100 million users. Since then, an average of 374,000 people have signed up every day. At this rate, Facebook will grow to nearly 300 million people by this time next year.

If you're reading this article, there's a good chance you already belong to Facebook. There's a good chance everyone you know is on Facebook, too. Indeed, there's a good chance you're no longer reading this article because you just switched over to check Facebook. That's fine—this piece is not for you. Instead I'd like to address those readers who aren't on Facebook, especially those of you who've consciously decided to stay away.

Though your ranks dwindle daily, there are many of you. This is understandable—any social movement that becomes so popular so fast engenders skepticism. A year ago, the *New York Observer* interviewed a half-dozen or so disdainful Facebook holdouts. "I don't see how having hundreds or thousands of 'friends' is leading to any kind of substantive friendships," said Cary Goldstein, the director of publicity at Twelve Publishers. "The whole thing seems so weird to me. Now you really have to turn off your computer and just go out to live real life and make real con-

Farhad Manjoo is a technology columnist for the New York Times *and the author of* True Enough.

Manjoo, Farhad. "You Have No Friends." *Slate.* 14 Jan. 2009. Web. 12 Mar. 2011. <http://www.slate.com/id/2208678>. © The Slate Group LLC.

nections with people that way. I don't think it's healthy." I was reminded of a quote from an *Onion* story, "Area Man Constantly Mentioning He Doesn't Own a Television": "I'm not an elitist. It's just that I'd much rather sculpt or write in my journal or read Proust than sit there passively staring at some phosphorescent screen."

Friends—can I call you friends?—it's time to drop the attitude: There is no longer any good reason to avoid Facebook. The site has crossed a threshold—it is now so widely trafficked that it's fast becoming a routine aid to social interaction, like e-mail and antiperspirant. It's only the most recent of many new technologies that have crossed over this stage. For a long while—from about the late '80s to the late-middle '90s, *Wall Street* to *Jerry Maguire*—carrying a mobile phone seemed like a haughty affectation. But as more people got phones, they became more useful for everyone—and then one day enough people had cell phones that everyone began to assume that you did, too. Your friends stopped prearranging where they would meet up on Saturday night because it was assumed that everyone would call from wherever they were to find out what was going on. From that moment on, it became an affectation *not* to carry a mobile phone; they'd grown so deeply entwined with modern life that the only reason to be without one was to make a statement by abstaining. Facebook is now at that same point—whether or not you intend it, you're saying something by staying away.

I use Facebook every day, and not always to waste time. Most of my extended family lives in South Africa, and though I speak to them occasionally on the phone, Facebook gives me an astonishingly intimate look at their lives—I can see what they did yesterday, what they're doing tomorrow, and what they're doing right now, almost like there's no distance separating us. The same holds true for my job: I live on the West Coast, but I work in an industry centered on the East Coast; Facebook gives me the opportunity to connect with people—to "network," you might say—in a completely natural, unaggressive manner. More than a dozen times, I've contacted sources through Facebook—searching for them there is much easier than searching for a current e-mail or phone number.

In fact, Facebook helped me write this story. The other day I posted a status update asking my Facebook friends to put me in touch with people who've decided against joining. The holdouts I contacted this way weren't haughty—they were nice, reasonable people with entirely rational-sounding explanations for staying off the site. Among the main reasons people cited was that Facebook looked like it required too much work. Chad Retelle, a network systems administrator in Madison, Wis., said he'd seen how his wife—my friend Katie—had taken to the site. But at the same time, it had changed her: "Now she's obligated to spend time maintaining her Facebook page. She's got to check it every morning. I have no desire to do that."

Retelle and other Facebook holdouts also protested that the site presents numerous opportunities for awkwardness—there's the headache of managing which people to friend and which to forget, the fear that one of your friends might post something on your wall that will offend everyone else, the worry that someone will find something about you that you didn't mean to share. Naomi Harris, a magazine photographer in New York, says that, for all that trouble, Facebook seems to offer little in return. "Why?" she asks. "I'm on the computer enough as it is for work. I don't really want to be there for recreation purposes, too. I have no interests in someone from fifth grade contacting me and saying, 'Hey, I sat behind you in class—wanna chat?' "

Finally, I heard what must be the most universal concern about Facebook—*I don't want people knowing my business!* Kate Koppelman is a 23-year-old New Yorker who works in the fashion industry. She was on Facebook all through college, and she concedes that the site has many benefits. And yet, the whole thing creeped her out: "I had friends from back home knowing what was going on with my friends from college—people they had never met—which was weird," she told me. "I found friends knowing things about what was on my 'wall' before I'd had a chance to see it—which was also weird." Koppelman quit Facebook last year. She still uses it by proxy—her roommates look people up for her when she's curious about them—but she says she'll never sign up again.

Yet of the many concerns about Facebook, Koppelman's is the most easily addressed. Last year, the site added a series of fine-grained privacy controls that let you choose which friends see what information about you. Your college friends can see one version of your profile, your high-school friends another, and your family yet another; if you want, you can let everyone see essentially nothing about you.

Retelle's worry that Facebook demands a lot of work is also somewhat misguided. It's true that some people spend a lot of time on it, but that's because they're having fun there; if you're not, you can simply log in once or twice a week just to accept or reject friends. Even doing nothing and waiting for others to friend you is enough: You're establishing a presence for other people to connect with you, which is the site's main purpose.

That brings us to Harris' argument: What's the social utility to Facebook—why should you join? Like with e-mail and cell phones, there are many, and as you begin to use it, you'll notice more and different situations in which it proves helpful. In general, Facebook is a lubricant of social connections. With so many people on it, it's now the best, fastest place online to find and connect with a specific person—think of it as a worldwide directory, or a Wikipedia of people. As a result, people now expect to find you on Facebook—whether they're contacting you for a job or scouting you out for a genius grant.

True, you might not want people to be able to follow your life—it's no great loss to you if your long-lost college frenemy can't find you. But what about your old fling, your new fling, your next employer, or that friend-of-a-friend you just met at a party who says he can give you some great tips on your golf swing? Sure, you can trade e-mail addresses or phone numbers, but in many circles Facebook is now the expected way to make these connections. By being on Facebook, you're facilitating such ties; without it, you're missing them and making life difficult for those who went looking for you there.

Skeptics often suggest that online social networks foster introverted, anti-social behavior—that we forge virtual connections at the expense of real-life connections. But only someone who's never used Facebook would make that argument. Nobody avoids meeting people in real life by escaping to the Web. In fact, the opposite seems true: Short, continuous, low-content updates about the particulars of your friends' lives—Bob has the flu, Barbara can't believe what just happened on *Mad Men,* Sally and Ned are no longer on speaking terms—deepen your bonds with them. Writer Clive Thompson has explored this phenomenon, what social scientists call "ambient awareness." Following someone through his status updates is not unlike sitting in a room with him and semiconsciously taking note of his body language, Thompson points out. Just as you can sense his mood from the rhythm of his breathing, sighing, and swearing, you can get the broad outlines of his life from short updates, making for a deeper conversation the next time you do meet up.

It's this benefit of Facebook that seems to hook people in the end: Their friendships seem to demand signing up. Last year, Darcy Stockton, a fashion photographer in New York, held nothing back in describing her hatred of Facebook to the *Observer.* "If you have time to network through a site like that, you aren't working enough," she said. "I just don't have the *time* or the *ability* to keep up with yet another social networking site in my free time. I feel there's other things and real experiences I could be having in real life instead of wasting my free time on Facebook."

Stockton now has 250 Facebook friends. In an e-mail, she explained that she'd decided to join the site when her friends migrated over from MySpace. She added, "Thank you for making me eat my words!"

Are We Facebook Friends Yet?

MICAH MCARTHUR

A common phrase exchanged among college students: "Are we Facebook friends yet?" As Facebook and other online social networks increase in popularity, the amount of time spent developing quality real-life relationships decreases. Every minute individuals spend socializing online is one minute they miss actually, physically socializing.

From a recent survey of students at Brigham Young University, 62 percent of the students who have a current Facebook account spend four to six hours every week logged in to their account, checking messages and updates or chatting. Nearly 10 percent of the students spend almost 18 hours/week logged in to their account—that's a part-time job! Many admit online social networking is addictive and feel they waste a lot of time online, but few follow through with the initial desire to change. They enjoy it too much and do not see the danger or the decline of their communication skills as they spend excessive amounts of time staring at a computer screen, "talking" with friends. Like other addictions, online social network users act on compulsion. When replaced with genuine, live relationships, the online friendship need dissolves, and one reverts back to the beauty of human relationships. This requires the user to spend time socializing in real life that they may have otherwise spent online.

Authentic personal interaction is becoming less common with the advances of technology and the convenience of impersonal communication. Elder David A. Bednar remarked in April this year: "Sadly, some young men and women ignore things as they really are and neglect eternal relationships for digital distractions, diversions and detours that have no lasting value. I am raising a warning voice that we should not squander and damage authentic relationships by obsessing over contrived ones."

Many of the students' "friends" were merely past acquaintances. Sometimes people are motivated to add friends from pity or guilt, rather than genuine interest in friendship. Better yet, some people have friend competitions to compare how many friends they have online.

McArthur, Micah. "Are We Facebook Friends Yet?" *The Universe.* 2 Dec. 2009. Web. 12 Mar. 2011. <http://www.universe.byu.edu/node/4570>. © Intellectual Reserve, Inc.

In addition, personal information shared online can cause unnecessary problems. There is a certain level of discretion many people have to figure out the hard way when using online social networks. Private issues need not be posted publicly. The one-line updates of thoughts or opinions these networks encourage are nothing more than generic information for the world to see—not the best personal contact or relationship building tool.

Another issue we face with a greater attention and interest in online social networking is anonymity—meeting people online who have never met in person before, as well as the being able to say whatever one feels with disregard for the consequences that would have followed.

Online chatting or commenting through Web sites like Twitter, Facebook, MySpace and Instant Messenger encourage anonymity, a sort of safety mask protecting the wearer from initial reactions, sarcasm and misinterpretations. Even for shy people, chatting via keyboard will only be a crutch that they will have to learn to live without once they leave the computer—if they leave the computer.

There are some friendships that time, distance or personal life cannot dispel. Online social networks can help individuals stay in contact with friends and family that they do not have time or means to communicate with in another way. The benefits of an online network ideally include availability to current information such as a phone number, address, e-mail or at least a means of getting one. Social networks can also provide alternative communication similar to e-mail as well as publication of announcements such as parties, social events and even business information.

The problem arises when users spend excessive time chatting online through these social networks instead of utilizing it as the great resource it could be. Users need to be aware of their purpose in using an online social network. Any excessive behavior can lead to addiction, but if used with discretion and proper awareness of long-term effects, users everywhere can benefit from the social networks found online and also enjoy quality friendships and communication in real life rather than online.

For the benefit of the future and for the sake of preserving the richness of culture, conversing through online chatting and social networks need to decrease authentic human communication such as quality face-to-face conversations, physical interactions among peers and true, bold, honest self expression needs to increase.

Why I Don't Watch What
My Kids Are Doing Online

Jody Allard

Earlier tonight, one of my teenage sons came home from his first date. He plopped down on the couch, kicked off his shoes, and told me pretty much everything. Not in graphic detail, thank God. But enough to know that he'd had his first kiss.

As we talked, we briefly discussed consent (in this case, his!), condoms, and his very firm belief that he isn't ready to have sex yet. After I shared a few condom tips I swear no one ever tells you until it's too late, he wandered off in search of food.

Later, my teenage daughter came in to tell me that her childhood BFF has started hanging out with kids who smoke pot. The girl's recent birthday party was a beach bonfire complete with weed. Even while proclaiming how stupid drugs are, and how sad it is her friends from middle school are doing drugs at age 14, my daughter paused to wonder why her BFF hadn't invited her. Exclusion hurts.

Later still, all three of my teens came together to discuss a mutual friend's living situation—they were concerned it might be unsafe.

After I finally managed to get everyone out of my bedroom, I replayed all of the evening's events. Sex, drugs, interpersonal relationships... But, I don't think that I have ever been as proud of my kids as I was tonight.

GOODBYE, STICKER CHARTS

I'm no expert at this parenting thing. I originally followed my own mother's approach simply because it was familiar and, I assumed, correct. But as my kids grew older—and I grew up—that approach evolved.

Originally, I had many rules, rewards, sticker charts, and punishments. My kids behaved pretty well, and I thought that I was an awesome parent. Then they hit their pre-teen years and started telling me all of the crazy things that they had been doing while I thought they were following the rules! Climbing out of windows and walking along the roof to get from their room to their sibling's room (just to get out of a time out!) was the one that really blew my mind. If my kids could swing that without me or my hyper-vigilant ex-husband noticing, it became clear that the idea of controlling my kids' behavior flat out didn't work.

NO MORE LIMITS

Since I'm not a fan of wasting my time, I tried something new. I ditched all of the rules, other than a few very basic ones that were written out and agreed to during a family meeting. I lifted all limits on screens. I got them smartphones. I made no effort to monitor their online behavior. I removed myself as a person of power and instead tried to create a new role of engaged leadership. I stopped lecturing so much and started listening more. And I kept talking to them about everything, from something I saw on Twitter to why I was touched by an article in the news. If I was concerned about their behavior, I talked to them about it, rather than creating a rule.

It's been two years now since I dramatically changed my parenting approach. Along the way, I found my own boundaries for what I was willing to accept from my kids, and I began to make that clear. There might not be many rules in our house, but I don't allow myself to be treated poorly, either. Thankfully, a sense of humor goes a long way toward easing tensions all around.

FACEBOOK FRIENDS SUGGEST STALKING

Recently, I've seen a surge in articles and social media posts about the need to monitor teens' behavior, especially online. A friend posted about the topic and her friends suggested everything from having all of her kids' emails forwarded to her, to viewing all of their friend's friend's friend's accounts on social media to see what kind of kids her kids hang out with. One mom reads her teens' texts every night. Another has software that monitors and tracks all internet usage.

When I encounter behavior like that among parents, I wonder why stalking your child is ever considered acceptable behavior. Stalking an adult is a crime. I don't understand why doing the same to a child has come to be considered good parenting.

A GREAT WAY TO WIN YOUR CHILD'S DISTRUST

I also have to ask myself what the goal is. Is it to protect kids from danger? Is it to make sure they never make a mistake? In any case, it seems designed to build resentment, distrust and hostility. Imagine how you would react if your significant other demanded you hand over copies of everything you did on your phone every day!

Kids have privacy and autonomy, too. By the time they reach the teen years, it's time for them to start making decisions, stretching those wings, and...making mistakes. Doing the same stupid stuff teens have been doing for decades. All in the name of being a flawed, imperfect human who learns and grows.

ERRING ON THE SIDE OF TRUST

My kids have generally been given as much freedom as I felt they could handle. In the past, I erred on the side of caution. Now, I err on the side of trust. Not because I expect them never to mess up, but because I want them to have the freedom to do just that while they are still safely cared for here at home.

Sometimes, I shake my head at the crazy things my kids do. But by being trusted to make their own choices, they have learned to trust themselves and their own judgment. Even at 16, for example, my oldest son doesn't want to learn how to drive. Instead, he takes the bus and has chosen to wait to drive until he feels ready.

I know that my kids won't always be on the "right" side of every situation, like they happened to be tonight. Eventually, they may choose to have sex or try pot. And, considering that 99% of the adults that I know have done both, I think that they will be just fine.

A few weeks ago, I de-friended my kids on Facebook. I realized that, with my kids as my friends, I just wasn't free to post openly. They were horrified by my decision, and gasped, almost in unison, "But, how will we know what's going on in your LIFE?!"

It's simple, I told them. You can ask.—J.A.

Bubbles Carry a Lot of Weight

JESSICA BENNETT

It's called the "typing awareness indicator," and a few months ago, my therapist ordered me to disable it on my phone. "It's causing you too much anxiety," she said, pointing to the iPhone I had in a white-knuckle grip. "It's giving monumental weight to matters of a text message."

But we weren't even talking about text messages ... exactly. We were talking about the time between text messages. Specifically that little gray bubble with the ellipses that pops up on your iPhone while the person on the other end of your text message is writing a response.

Or, in my case—in the particularly high-stakes conversation at hand—it was the bubble that popped up to indicate typing, then disappeared to show he had stopped. Then came back up to show typing, then went away again. Then returned for what seemed like an eternity (he must be writing something deep, right?) only to produce a response so benign (you know, like "cool" or "ya") that it could only be topped by the humiliation of the bubble never returning at all (meaning he was flat-out ignoring me). Which I would know, of course, because I could see that he had read my message (that's called a "read receipt").

"The three dots shown while someone is drafting a message in iMessage is quite possibly the most important source of eternal hope and ultimate letdown in our daily lives," said Maryam Abolfazli, a writer in Washington who has tackled the topic. "It's the modern-day version of watching paint dry, except you might be broken up with by the time the dots deliver."

For some time, sociologists have studied the way that new technology affects the brain; the way that constant updates prime us to fear we're missing out, or the way we crave the adrenaline rush brought on by a constant stream of digital micro-communications.

But what about the tyranny of the text bubble? Indeed, there are real problems in the world. But this was the kind of modern-day technological minutiae that had the ability to jail me in a very specific cognitive hell.

"The awareness indicator as implemented on the iPhone is a curious beast—it conveys that something is being done, but it won't say what," said Paul Dourish, a professor at the University of California, Irvine, who studies the intersection of technology and society. "It's curiously coy."

I've taken to calling this the "so and so is typing" feature, as does the man who invented it for the iPhone—a close relative of, but not to be confused with, the "delivered" status and "read receipt," also staples of modern texting.

The specifics of the feature vary slightly based on the platform. On an iPhone, the bubble appears when you're messaging another iPhone user; on desktop clients like Google Chat or Facebook Messenger, you'll receive a "Jessica is typing ... " blurb. But whatever form it takes, it remains, as my friend Ben Crair put it in a recent essay in the New Republic, "the most awkward part of online chat."

The roots of the typing awareness indicator go back to the 1990s, when people used dial-up (the horror!). But back then, it had a practical purpose: It let you know when a person was online, or that a message was delivered. Remember the old AOL Buddy List? As the Wired columnist Clive Thompson reminded me, it was perhaps the first popular iteration of this system: a creaking door noise to notify you when a friend signed on, and a door slamming when he or she left.

But it wasn't until 2005 that BlackBerry became the first big company to bring the "delivered," "read" and "so and so is typing" features to mobile with BlackBerry Messenger, or BBM. Two years later, Apple introduced the iPhone with SMS, and four years after that, iMessage, which added a real-time element to otherwise jilted conversations.

As technologists describe it, the typing feature rests somewhere between real-life speech, with tone and pacing—what linguists call "synchronous" communication—and text-based communication ("asynchronous"), which occurs in spurts, out of sync, like email. "It's like eye contact in a conversation: You know if they're paying attention," said Gary Klassen, the principal architect at BlackBerry and the lead developer of BBM.

And yet, while desktop communication still comes with the question "Are you there?" on mobile, presence isn't just expected—it's mandatory. So the typing indicator has become a message in and of itself, "the equivalent of saying, 'Hold on, I'm responding,' " said Ron Palmeri, the founder of a communications start-up called Layer that specializes in chat technology.

Or ... "I'm not responding."

Which brings us back to text-bubble anxiety, of which there are many forms.

There's the text bubble of the highly charged emotional conversation (also known "Aaaah, this next could dictate everything!") that really shouldn't be happening over text message in the first place but is because, well, that's the way we communicate these days.

There's the giving-away-too-much-without-actually-saying-anything pause, when you start to type and then decide to edit your response. ("You know I can see you typing, right?" a friend recently said to me, as I fumbled over an answer for whether I was mad at her.)

There are the times when the iPhone has actually malfunctioned and you have just worked yourself into a rage for no reason, or the times you blindly convince yourself that it has. "I've found this self-delusion quite helpful," said Sally Kohn, a political commentator.

Or there's the text you want to pretend you haven't read yet—but then find that your pocket has pressed against the cursor, which is now in the response tab and, damn, now he knows that you've seen it and your whole plan is foiled.

Laura Barganier, a public relations manager in New York, told me recently, "Sometimes I don't want someone—O.K., likely a boy—to know I'm taking so long to write a text that I start a brand-new blank text and then copy and paste it in the original chain,"

"But don't you wonder if he wonders how you typed so quickly?" I asked.

"I fake type for a few seconds," she responded.

As Neal Bledsoe, an actor in Los Angeles, put it (over text message, naturally): "This is the new human condition. We're all desperate for human connection, and all we get—after all that typing—is a paper-clip emoji."

This Is How to Stalk Your Teenage Children Online

BELINDA LUSCOMBE

I knew I had to be very careful when choosing a fake online identity with which to stalk my kids. It needed to be somebody that my children would want to be friends with, but not close friends, somebody who might plausibly notice them, but they might not notice being noticed by.

That's how I ended up becoming Clara Lemlich. She was a leader of a massive strike of female shirtwaist workers in New York City more than a century ago. Logically, a modern Clara would be interested in clothes and young women, exactly what both my teenagers are interested in.

It's well-known that only loser teenagers befriend people who don't already have friends so I rounded out Clara's profile by prefriending a whole bunch of people I knew my kids (a 13 year old girl and 16 year old boy) would find cool. That noted labor organizer, Channing Tatum, for example.

Given Ms. Lemlich's areas of expertise, it's not weird or creepy or anything that my children might crop up on her radar. Well, perhaps it's a little creepy. I mean, if I were their mother and I saw some random adult pretending to be a dead union activist looking at their photos on Instagram, I'd be alarmed. But I am their mother, so …..anyway, I digress.

My ruse made just enough sense that when Clara Lemlich started following my kids, she seemed both acceptable and ignorable; they took the bait. Online friends are after all, more desirable for their quantity than their quality. The only person my children do not want to add to their list of followers is me.

Surely, you're saying, there's some more upfront, reasonable, less sneaky way to do this. Experts recommend, for example, that you have all your children's passwords and make sure that you have full access to all their social media sites. To which I say: bwahahahahaha. Good luck. You

Luscombe, Belinda. "This Is How to Stalk Your Teenage Children Online." *Time*. Time, Inc. 20 Oct. 2014. <http://time.com/3523213/men-women-and-children-internet-safe-ty-kids/>. © Time, Inc.

will never get ahead of your teenagers on nefarious uses of technology. I'll wager young Rory Gates has already figured out at least one way to digitally outsmart his dad, Bill.

In the new movie *Men, Women & Children,* Jennifer Garner plays a mom trying to do exactly what those parenting gurus recommend. She has all her daughter's passwords. She tracks her daughter on her iPhone. Her computer records every website the girl has visited, every text her phone receives and every person who texts her, just to make sure there are no predators. (Her daughter goes along with all of this, because her daughter is a completely fictional construct.)

I'm not worried about predators. I pity any poor perv who tries to get my kids off the couch. But like Garner's character Patricia, I do worry that what the kids are posting might blow back on them later. As Patricia says: "our children will be the first generation whose lives have a searchable database."

That's why I felt I needed Clara Lemlich. The Internet is too vast and labyrinthine to be mapped. Parents can't give their offspring a guidebook or a list of dangerous neighborhoods, even if they knew them. They can't warn them ahead of time to avoid doing something that might later seem terrible. But this public vast world is also holdable in one hand; It's as if their bus pass could allow them to time travel. And strip when they get there.

But once I had successfully Trojan horsed my way into my kids's online lives, I found their cities somewhat lacking in drama. There were no fights to join. Their activities mostly consist of friends being excessively complimentary of each other and excessively unpleasant about strangers. It's narcissistic but not dangerous. The biggest infraction my daughter seems to be guilty of is copyright infringement: she's posting photos I took. Without attribution.

So I'm outing Clara Lemlich. Hi kids, it's me. Isn't this Instagram thing fun? Of course, they don't follow me on social media, so they'll never know.

Re: Our Relationship

EMMA PIERSON

As a scientist who studies online-dating data, I've spent a lot of time quantifying how other people fall in love. I began to wonder whether it was possible to apply the same methods to my own relationship. I told myself it was for the sake of science: I was acting out of professional curiosity, and would understand others' relationships better by putting myself under the mathematical microscope.

But it would be more honest to admit it was also because I missed my boyfriend. After spending three years at college with him, I had left to study for a year at Oxford; this was my equivalent of flipping through photo albums.

But what data to use? We rarely text or take pictures. But in the four years since we began dating, we've exchanged an average of four emails a day, which works out to more than 5,500 emails. If we had just typed out literature to each other, we would've recently completed *Harry Potter and the Goblet of Fire,* though we won't finish *Infinite Jest* for another six years or *In Search of Lost Time* for another 19. When I told my boyfriend I wanted to statistically analyze our emails, we had the following conversation:

Him: I think you should ask my permission to do that.
Me: I wouldn't ask your permission to read the emails. Why should reading them using a computer be any different?
Him: You're going to find some weird pattern and break up with me.
Me: Either that will be warranted by the data, in which case it's a good thing, or it won't, in which case I'm a bad statistician. Are you saying I'm a bad statistician?

This is what scientists call "obtaining consent."

It was dark and drizzling when I walked back alone to my Oxford dorm room, curled up around my laptop, and dove into the digital record of our relationship. I was unsurprised to find that our emails became more frequent after I left for England. But I felt a jolt when I discovered that I sent my boyfriend far more emails than he sent me.

I closed my program, made myself a cup of tea, called my boyfriend, and asked him why, according to the data, I missed him more than he missed me. He said that wasn't true, he just preferred to talk on the phone rather than send me emails. I went back to the data to see if it substantiated his claim, and indeed it did: He used "call me" and "phone" more frequently in his emails.

Having avoided one potential breakup, I returned to the data and looked at how the average length of our emails changed over time. I found large spikes corresponding to the first three times we were apart for our university's spring, summer, and winter breaks. These lengthy emails turned out to be, unsurprisingly, the sort of pour-your-soul-out messages that accompany first infatuation. The content of the emails changed over time in other ways as well. For example, we used the word "promise" more frequently early in our relationship, often to make the sort of charming but trivial pledges that build trust—"I promise not to kill you," or "I promise never to make you go to a yacht club." On the other hand, we began to use nicknames and endearments only later in our relationship—promises replaced by pet names.

Then I wondered if differences in our personalities would show up in our emails. I compared the words I used with the words he used; this revealed that, contrary to gender stereotypes, I am probably more aggressive. I am responsible, for example, for more than 95 percent of the profanity in our emails. He is much more likely to use the phrase "I am not sure," and is also responsible for 60 percent of the incidences of "sorry." I have a penchant for bleaker topics, and am more likely to mention "pain," "cancer," and "suicide." I am also more likely to make sweeping generalizations about men, as evidenced by my more frequent use of "boys" and "male."

We each bring up our interests: He, the quadrilinguist, mentions Greek, Latin, and Italian. I use words related to statistics. Our language is distinctive in other ways. He, the New Englander, is much more likely to use the word "dandy" (as in Yankee Doodle); I, who when comfortable with someone begin talking like a frat boy, am much more likely to use the word "bro."

To avoid getting dumped, I will stop sharing details of our emails and will instead share two larger lessons I learned about love. The first is that statistics can be unexpectedly, painfully powerful. I had long known the joy of slicing out truth with a statistical scalpel, but here the heart I'd cut into was my own. Why does my boyfriend apologize more than I do? Why have our emails gotten shorter? What if I still want promises, not just pet names? Another statistician of love, the founder of the dating site OkCupid, once said that analyzing people's relationships made him "very grim" because he had to "embrace the darkness." I always found this a bit melodramatic, but perhaps he simply empathized better than I did with the lovers who went under his knife.

I was originally planning to make an app to allow anyone to analyze their own relationship, but it isn't clear to me I'd be offering something worth having. There are far more unpleasant things you could find. What if your partner's emails are less affectionate on days when they have meetings with that attractive co-worker? What if you no longer send them flirtatious emails, or only tell them they're attractive after 10 p.m. on Fridays and Saturdays, when you tend to be drinking? What if you discussed Plato and Proust with your ex, and with your current partner you only talk about what's for dinner? (I did not perform a comparative analysis across my relationships because I figured my exes dislike me enough already.)

You might argue that if these things are true, it is better to be aware of them. But I am not sure that love is best looked at so clear-eyed. Relationships are weird: *pas de deux* that in the moment are endearing seem bizarre when coldly quantified; full of truths that might be softer if only dimly perceived. If you never thought of your partner as unaffectionate until you learned they say "I love you" 20 percent less frequently than you do, what benefit have you gained?

The second lesson I learned is about the limits of statistics. My relationship is not fully captured by my emails: What I remember are the moments themselves, not their digital shadows. The entire email record of my relationship can itself be attached to an email. It is but a hundredth of a hundredth of a hard drive, a pinch of electron fairydust that cannot contain four years of tears and touches. And my emails are not fully captured by my algorithms, which would react the same way if I took every carefully crafted message and scrambled the words into random order. Writing this piece alone, what I want is my boyfriend; what I have are some line graphs. If I lose this much when I study a single relationship on which I'm an expert, God knows what I'm losing when I apply the same approach to tens of thousands of people I've never met.

So those are the twin and opposite warnings I'd pass on to those who would reduce love to a line graph: You don't know what you're missing, and you don't know what you'll find. Perhaps the moments that count most can't—or shouldn't—be counted.

Digital Culture

The Amorality of Web 2.0

NICHOLAS CARR

From the start, the World Wide Web has been a vessel of quasi-religious longing. And why not? For those seeking to transcend the physical world, the Web presents a readymade Promised Land. On the Internet, we're all bodiless, symbols speaking to symbols in symbols. The early texts of Web metaphysics, many written by thinkers associated with or influenced by the post-60s New Age movement, are rich with a sense of impending spiritual release; they describe the passage into the cyber world as a process of personal and communal unshackling, a journey that frees us from traditional constraints on our intelligence, our communities, our meager physical selves. We become free-floating netizens in a more enlightened, almost angelic, realm.

But as the Web matured during the late 1990s, the dreams of a digital awakening went unfulfilled. The Net turned out to be more about commerce than consciousness, more a mall than a commune. And when the new millenium arrived, it brought not a new age but a dispiritingly commonplace popping of a bubble of earthly greed. Somewhere along the way, the moneychangers had taken over the temple. The Internet had transformed many things, but it had not transformed us. We were the same as ever.

THE NEW NEW AGE

But the yearning for a higher consciousness didn't burst with the bubble. Web 1.0 may have turned out to be spiritual vaporware, but now we have the hyper-hyped upgrade: Web 2.0. In a profile of Internet savant Tim O'Reilly in the current issue of Wired, Steven Levy writes that "the idea of collective consciousness is becoming manifest in the Internet." He quotes O'Reilly: "The Internet today is so much an echo of what we were talking about at [New Age HQ] Esalen in the '70s—except we didn't know it would be technology-mediated." Levy then asks, "Could it be

Carr, Nicholas. "The Amorality of Web 2.0." *Rough Type*. Blog post. 3 Oct. 2005. Web. 12 Mar. 2011. © Nicholas Carr.

that the Internet—or what O'Reilly calls Web 2.0—is really the successor to the human potential movement?"

Levy's article appears in the afterglow of Kevin Kelly's sweeping "We Are the Web" in Wired's August issue. Kelly, erstwhile prophet of the Long Boom, surveys the development of the World Wide Web, from the Netscape IPO ten years ago, and concludes that it has become a "magic window" that provides a "spookily godlike" perspective on existence. "I doubt angels have a better view of humanity," he writes.

But that's only the beginning. In the future, according to Kelly, the Web will grant us not only the vision of gods but also their power. The Web is becoming "the OS for a megacomputer that encompasses the Internet, all its services, all peripheral chips and affiliated devices from scanners to satellites, and the billions of human minds entangled in this global network. This gargantuan Machine already exists in a primitive form. In the coming decade, it will evolve into an integral extension not only of our senses and bodies but our minds ... We will live inside this thing."

The revelation continues:

> There is only one time in the history of each planet when its inhabitants first wire up its innumerable parts to make one large Machine. Later that Machine may run faster, but there is only one time when it is born.
>
> You and I are alive at this moment.
>
> We should marvel, but people alive at such times usually don't. Every few centuries, the steady march of change meets a discontinuity, and history hinges on that moment. We look back on those pivotal eras and wonder what it would have been like to be alive then. Confucius, Zoroaster, Buddha, and the latter Jewish patriarchs lived in the same historical era, an inflection point known as the axial age of religion. Few world religions were born after this time. Similarly, the great personalities converging upon the American Revolution and the geniuses who commingled during the invention of modern science in the 17th century mark additional axial phases in the short history of our civilization.
>
> Three thousand years from now, when keen minds review the past, I believe that our ancient time, here at the cusp of the third millennium, will be seen as another such era. In the years roughly coincidental with the Netscape IPO, humans began animating inert objects with tiny slivers of intelligence, connecting them into a global field, and linking their own minds into a single thing. This will be recognized as the largest, most complex,

and most surprising event on the planet. Weaving nerves out of glass and radio waves, our species began wiring up all regions, all processes, all facts and notions into a grand network. From this embryonic neural net was born a collaborative interface for our civilization, a sensing, cognitive device with power that exceeded any previous invention. The Machine provided a new way of thinking (perfect search, total recall) and a new mind for an old species. It was the Beginning.

This isn't the language of exposition. It's the language of rapture.

THE CULT OF THE AMATEUR

Now, lest you dismiss me as a mere cynic, if not a fallen angel, let me make clear that I'm all for seeking transcendence, whether it's by going to church or living in a hut in the woods or sitting at the feet of the Maharishi or gazing into the glittering pixels of an LCD screen. One gathers one's manna where one finds it. And if there's a higher consciousness to be found, then by all means let's get elevated. My problem is this: When we view the Web in religious terms, when we imbue it with our personal yearning for transcendence, we can no longer see it objectively. By necessity, we have to look at the Internet as a moral force, not as a simple collection of inanimate hardware and software. No decent person wants to worship an amoral conglomeration of technology.

And so all the things that Web 2.0 represents—participation, collectivism, virtual communities, amateurism—become unarguably good things, things to be nurtured and applauded, emblems of progress toward a more enlightened state. But is it really so? Is there a counterargument to be made? Might, on balance, the practical effect of Web 2.0 on society and culture be bad, not good? To see Web 2.0 as a moral force is to turn a deaf ear to such questions.

Let me bring the discussion down to a brass tack. If you read anything about Web 2.0, you'll inevitably find praise heaped upon Wikipedia as a glorious manifestation of "the age of participation." Wikipedia is an open-source encyclopedia; anyone who wants to contribute can add an entry or edit an existing one. O'Reilly, in a new essay on Web 2.0, says that Wikipedia marks "a profound change in the dynamics of content creation"—a leap beyond the Web 1.0 model of Britannica Online. To Kevin Kelly, Wikipedia shows how the Web is allowing us to pool our individual brains into a great collective mind. It's a harbinger of the Machine.

In theory, Wikipedia is a beautiful thing—it has to be a beautiful thing if the Web is leading us to a higher consciousness. In reality, though, Wikipedia isn't very good at all. Certainly, it's useful—I regularly consult it to get a quick gloss on a subject. But at a factual level it's unreliable, and the writing is often appalling. I wouldn't depend on it as a source, and I certainly wouldn't recommend it to a student writing a research paper.

Take, for instance, this section from Wikipedia's biography of Bill Gates, excerpted verbatim:

> Gates married Melinda French on January 1, 1994. They have three children, Jennifer Katharine Gates (born April 26, 1996), Rory John Gates (born May 23, 1999) and Phoebe Adele Gates (born September 14, 2002).
>
> In 1994, Gates acquired the Codex Leicester, a collection of writings by Leonardo da Vinci; as of 2003 it was on display at the Seattle Art Museum.
>
> In 1997, Gates was the victim of a bizarre extortion plot by Chicago resident Adam Quinn Pletcher. Gates testified at the subsequent trial. Pletcher was convicted and sentenced in July 1998 to six years in prison. In February 1998 Gates was attacked by Noël Godin with a cream pie. In July 2005, he solicited the services of famed lawyer Hesham Foda.
>
> According to Forbes, Gates contributed money to the 2004 presidential campaign of George W. Bush. According to the Center for Responsive Politics, Gates is cited as having contributed at least $33,335 to over 50 political campaigns during the 2004 election cycle.

Excuse me for stating the obvious, but this is garbage, an incoherent hodge-podge of dubious factoids (who the heck is "famed lawyer Hesham Foda"?) that adds up to something far less than the sum of its parts.

Here's Wikipedia on Jane Fonda's life, again excerpted verbatim:

> Her nickname as a youth—Lady Jane—was one she reportedly disliked. She traveled to Communist Russia in 1964 and was impressed by the people, who welcomed her warmly as Henry's daughter. In the mid-1960s she bought a farm outside of Paris, had it renovated and personally started a garden. She visited Andy Warhol's Factory in 1966. About her 1971 Oscar win, her father Henry said: "How in hell would you like to have been in this business as long as I and have one of your kids win an Oscar before you do?" Jane was on the cover of Life magazine, March 29, 1968.
>
> While early she had grown both distant from and critical

of her father for much of her young life, in 1980, she bought the play "On Golden Pond" for the purpose of acting alongside her father—hoping he might win the Oscar that had eluded him throughout his career. He won, and when she accepted the Oscar on his behalf, she said it was "the happiest night of my life." Director and first husband Roger Vadim once said about her: "Living with Jane was difficult in the beginning ... she had so many, how do you say, 'bachelor habits.' Too much organization. Time is her enemy. She cannot relax. Always there is something to do." Vadim also said, "There is also in Jane a basic wish to carry things to the limit."

This is worse than bad, and it is, unfortunately, representative of the slipshod quality of much of Wikipedia. Remember, this emanation of collective intelligence is not just a couple of months old. It's been around for nearly five years and has been worked over by many thousands of diligent contributors. At this point, it seems fair to ask exactly when the intelligence in "collective intelligence" will begin to manifest itself. When will the great Wikipedia get good? Or is "good" an old-fashioned concept that doesn't apply to emergent phenomena like communal on-line encyclopedias?

The promoters of Web 2.0 venerate the amateur and distrust the professional. We see it in their unalloyed praise of Wikipedia, and we see it in their worship of open-source software and myriad other examples of democratic creativity. Perhaps nowhere, though, is their love of amateurism so apparent as in their promotion of blogging as an alternative to what they call "the mainstream media." Here's O'Reilly: "While mainstream media may see individual blogs as competitors, what is really unnerving is that the competition is with the blogosphere as a whole. This is not just a competition between sites, but a competition between business models. The world of Web 2.0 is also the world of what Dan Gillmor calls 'we, the media,' a world in which 'the former audience,' not a few people in a back room, decides what's important."

I'm all for blogs and blogging. (I'm writing this, ain't I?) But I'm not blind to the limitations and the flaws of the blogosphere—its superficiality, its emphasis on opinion over reporting, its echolalia, its tendency to reinforce rather than challenge ideological extremism and segregation. Now, all the same criticisms can (and should) be hurled at segments of the mainstream media. And yet, at its best, the mainstream media is able to do things that are different from—and, yes, more important than—what bloggers can do. Those despised "people in a back room" can fund in-depth reporting and research. They can underwrite projects that can take months or years to reach fruition—or that may fail altogether. They can hire and pay talented people who would not be able to survive as sole proprietors on the Internet. They can employ editors and proofreaders and other unsung protectors of quality work. They can place, with equal weight, opposing ideologies on the same page. Forced to choose between reading blogs and subscribing to, say, the New York Times, the Financial Times, the Atlantic, and the Economist, I will choose the latter. I will take the professionals over the amateurs.

But I don't want to be forced to make that choice.

SCARY ECONOMICS

And so, having gone on for so long, I at long last come to my point. The Internet is changing the economics of creative work—or, to put it more broadly, the economics of culture—and it's doing it in a way that may well restrict rather than expand our choices. Wikipedia might be a pale shadow of the Britannica, but because it's created by amateurs rather than professionals, it's free. And free trumps quality all the time. So what happens to those poor saps who write encyclopedias for a living? They wither and die. The same thing happens when blogs and other free on-line content go up against old-fashioned newspapers and magazines. Of course the mainstream media sees the blogosphere as a competitor. It is a competitor. And, given the economics of the competition, it may well turn out to be a superior competitor. The layoffs we've recently seen at major newspapers may just be the beginning, and those layoffs should be cause not for self-satisfied snickering but for despair. Implicit in the ecstatic visions of Web 2.0 is the hegemony of the amateur. I for one can't imagine anything more frightening.

In "We Are the Web," Kelly writes that "because of the ease of creation and dissemination, online culture is *the culture*." I hope he's wrong, but I fear he's right—or will come to be right.

Like it or not, Web 2.0, like Web 1.0, is amoral. It's a set of technologies—a machine, not a Machine—that alters the forms and economics of production and consumption. It doesn't care whether its consequences are good or bad. It doesn't care whether it brings us to a higher consciousness or a lower one. It doesn't care whether it burnishes our culture or dulls it. It doesn't care whether it leads us into a golden age or a dark one. So let's can the millenialist rhetoric and see the thing for what it is, not what we wish it would be.

The People Formerly Known as the Audience

JAY ROSEN

The people formerly known as the audience wish to inform media people of our existence, and of a shift in power that goes with the platform shift you've all heard about.

Think of passengers on your ship who got a boat of their own. The writing readers. The viewers who picked up a camera. The formerly atomized listeners who with modest effort can connect with each other and gain the means to speak—to the world, as it were.

Now we understand that met with ringing statements like these many media people want to cry out in the name of reason herself: If all would speak who shall be left to listen? Can you at least tell us that?

The people formerly known as the audience do not believe this problem—too many speakers!—is our problem. Now for anyone in your circle still wondering who we are, a formal definition might go like this:

The people formerly known as the audience are those who were on the receiving end of a media system that ran one way, in a broadcasting pattern, with high entry fees and a few firms competing to speak very loudly while the rest of the population listened in isolation from one another—and who today are not in a situation like that at all.

- Once they were your printing presses; now that humble device, the blog, has given the press to us. That's why blogs have been called little First Amendment machines. They extend freedom of the press to more actors.

- Once it was your radio station, broadcasting on your frequency. Now that brilliant invention, podcasting, gives radio to us. And we have found more uses for it than you did.

- Shooting, editing and distributing video once belonged to you, Big

Media. Only you could afford to reach a TV audience built in your own image. Now video is coming into the user's hands, and audience-building by former members of the audience is alive and well on the Web.

- You were once (exclusively) the editors of the news, choosing what ran on the front page. Now we can edit the news, and our choices send items to our own front pages.
- A highly centralized media system had connected people "up" to big social agencies and centers of power but not "across" to each other. Now the horizontal flow, citizen-to-citizen, is as real and consequential as the vertical one.

The "former audience" is Dan Gillmor's term for us. (He's one of our discoverers and champions.) It refers to the owners and operators of tools that were once exclusively used by media people to capture and hold their attention.

Jeff Jarvis, a former media executive, has written a law about us. "Give the people control of media, they will use it. The corollary: Don't give the people control of media, and you will lose. Whenever citizens can exercise control, they will."

Look, media people. We are still perfectly content to listen to our radios while driving, sit passively in the darkness of the local multiplex, watch TV while motionless and glassy-eyed in bed, and read silently to ourselves as we always have.

Should we attend the theatre, we are unlikely to storm the stage for purposes of putting on our own production. We feel there is nothing wrong with old style, one-way, top-down media consumption. Big Media pleasures will not be denied us. You provide them, we'll consume them and you can have yourselves a nice little business.

But we're not on your clock any more. Tom Curley, CEO of the Associated Press, has explained this to his people. "The users are deciding what the point of their engagement will be—what application, what device, what time, what place."

We graduate from wanting media when we want it, to wanting it without the filler, to wanting media to be way better than it is, to publishing and broadcasting ourselves when it meets a need or sounds like fun.

Mark Thompson, director general of the BBC, has a term for us: The Active Audience ("who doesn't want to just sit there but to take part, debate, create, communicate, share.")

Another of your big shots, Rupert Murdoch, told American newspaper editors about us: "They want control over their media, instead of being controlled by it."

Dave Winer, one of the founders of blogging, said it back in 1994: "Once the users take control, they never give it back."

Online, we tend to form user communities around our favorite spaces. Tom Glocer, head of your Reuters, recognized it: "If you want to attract a community around you, you must offer them something original and of a quality that they can react to and incorporate in their creative work."

We think you're getting the idea, media people. If not from us, then from your own kind describing the same shifts.

The people formerly known as the audience would like to say a special word to those working in the media who, in the intensity of their commercial vision, had taken to calling us "eyeballs," as in: "There is always a new challenge coming along for the eyeballs of our customers." (John Fithian, president of the National Association of Theater Owners in the U.S.)

Or: "We already own the eyeballs on the television screen. We want to make sure we own the eyeballs on the computer screen." (Ann Kirschner, vice president for programming and media development for the National Football League.)

Fithian, Kirschner and company should know that such fantastic delusions ("we own the eyeballs...") were the historical products of a media system that gave its operators an exaggerated sense of their own power and mastery over others. New media is undoing all that, which makes us smile.

You don't own the eyeballs. You don't own the press, which is now divided into pro and amateur zones. You don't control production on the new platform, which isn't one-way. There's a new balance of power between you and us.

The people formerly known as the audience are simply the public made realer, less fictional, more able, less predictable. You should welcome that, media people. But whether you do or not, we want you to know we're here.

When My Kids Unplugged

SUSAN MAUSHART

There were lots of reasons why we pulled the plug on my family's electronic media for six months ... or, I should say, why I did, because heaven knows my children would have sooner volunteered to go without food, water or hair products. At ages fourteen, fifteen and eighteen, my daughters and my son don't use media. They *inhabit* media. And they do so exactly as a fish inhabits a pond. Gracefully. Unblinkingly. And utterly without consciousness or curiosity as to how they got there. Over a period of years, I watched and worried as our media began to function as a force field separating my children from what my son, only half-ironically, called RL (Real Life). But to be honest, the teenagers weren't the only ones with dependency issues. Although a recent arrival to the global village, I'd been known to abuse information too.

And clearly, we weren't alone. Zeynep Tufekci, who teaches sociology to students at the University of Maryland, is convinced that social-networking media are making us more, not less, accountable for our actions. "We're going back to a more normal place, historically," she observes—a place not unlike a small town, where everybody knows your business, whether you want them to or not. Identity theft is no longer the issue, Tufekci argues—but preserving anonymity may well be. "You know that old cartoon? On the Internet, nobody knows you're a dog? On the Internet today, everybody knows you're a dog. If you don't want people to know you're a dog, you'd better stay away from a keyboard."

Other observers worry that our meaningful relationships are being nudged aside by one-sided "parasocial" connections, such as my fourteen-year-old daughter Sussy's relationship with Taylor Swift or Zooey Deschanel: "Peripheral people in our network whose intimate details we follow closely online, even while they ... are basically unaware we exist," in

Susan Maushart is a writer living on Long Island, New York and the author of "The Mask of Motherhood" and "The Winter of Our Disconnect."

Maushart, Susan. "When My Kids Unplugged." *Salon.* 22 Jan. 2011. Web. 17 Mar. 2011. <http://www.salon.com/life/feature/2011/01/22/winter_of_disconnect/index.html>.

the words of Danah Boyd, a fellow at Harvard's Berman Center for Internet and Society. Social media have enabled an explosion of what anthropologists call "weak ties." But whither the strong ones? The deep ones?

And speaking of getting real, Flickr cofounder Caterina Fake—and no, I am not making that up—admitted recently that the ease of online sharing has made her slack about getting together with friends the old-fashioned way, in high-resolution reality. "These technologies allow you to be much more broadly friendly, but you just spread yourself much more thinly over many more people," she explained. And who wants to raise a stack of pancake people (to use playwright Richard Foreman's term for those who are becoming—as it were—flattened by Facebook)? My worst fear as a parent was that my kids might lose an alternative frame of reference—that growing up as Digital Natives, they would swallow the pancake paradigm whole and forget there were more nourishing ways for friends and family to connect.

One particular evening my daughter Sussy and I hunkered down in front of the fire with the boxes of family photos ("Whoa. Look at all those hard copies!" she cried) for a veritable festival of face-to-Facebook-ing was a good case in point. We devoured thousands of images, laughing, hooting, or blinking in wonderment just as we would have done online. But sitting side by side, passing pictures from one set of hands to another, created a different energy. We didn't simply consume the images, or allow them to consume us. Rather, they became catapults, triggers for stories and recollections, for the exchange of family and cultural history far greater than the sum of the individual parts. "Yes, darling, Grammy was a hottie back in sixty-nine," I agreed, my eyes bright with unshed tears. "No, I'm pretty sure that was her real hair."

An impromptu glee club I encountered on one summer night around the piano evoked similar longings: more than a nostalgia for the real, it was a déjà vu about the real, I reflected, as the playlist skidded freakily from "The Jungle Book" to Death Cab for Cutie and back again. "I had no idea [your friend] could play the piano!" I exclaimed to my eighteen-year-old daughter Anni after the group dispersed that night. "To be honest, neither did I," she admitted.

"Was it okay? I mean, you all looked like you were having fun ..." I trailed off.

"Fun?" she spat back. "You must be joking! It was awesome."

My fifteen-year-old son Bill's exile from MSN, Facebook, and his anime stash propelled him out of the door faster than a bullet from one of his beloved first-person shooter games. My dread was that he would simply make a beeline for his friend's house. And he did too—at first. Within a week or two, his separation anxiety seemed to dissipate. He started spending more time at the beach and pool, catching up with friends he hadn't connected with since primary school. Matt, for instance, who was now a serious trumpet player, and Tom, the older brother of Bill's gaming buddy Pat, who had recently taken up jazz piano. They were both studying with the same teacher, a saxophonist named Paul Andrews, Bill reported. And so began the prelude to his renewed interest in the saxophone. Any chance that he could start lessons again? he asked me soon afterward.

I pretended to consider it—no sense ruining everything by showing my approval—and agreed to a "trial lesson." I came in at the end of it, just in time to see Andrews nod his head curtly.

"So, tell me. What do you want to be?"

"A musician," Bill replied without hesitation.

("WTF?" I was screaming internally.)

"Uh huh." Andrews nodded again. "Well, practice, focus, listen, learn ... and you can be."

Up to that point, Bill had barely picked up his instrument in two years. From that point, he has hardly put it down.

In the ensuing weeks and months after that pivotal first lesson, I watched my son evolve like a human Pokémon from a surly, back-talking gamer to a surly back-talking musician in-the-making. (LOL.) To this day, Bill insists that it wasn't the technology ban that changed him. It was the friends, and the teacher they'd led him to. "Ah. I see," I reply.

"The technology ban was nothing but a trigger," he adds, a little less certainly.

"Ah, a trigger," I echo. (Bang, bang! I think to myself. Got 'im!)

Sussy ended up switching friendship groups too. Loss of Facebook (not to mention loss of MSN and MySpace) seemed to increase her focus generally; at the same time, it put her out of the loop with her old friends. "With Jen and Cat and that kind of group, you figure stuff out on the computer, like sleepovers and stuff," she explained to me. These invitations happened spontaneously, usually on the spur of the moment, in fact, with little or no notice. If you blinked—or, more to the point, if you went offline—you missed them. The girls in Sussy's new group at school didn't operate like that. "We planned a sleepover a week in advance!" she told me proudly, and slightly incredulously.

Sussy's coping mechanisms differed from Anni's and Bill's significantly. The older kids took the opportunity to go out more—shopping, visiting, or clubbing in Anni's case, and hanging out at the pool or jamming in somebody's garage in Bill's. Sussy had fewer friends who lived in the neighborhood, so she faced major transportation issues. Her best girlfriend, my goddaughter Maddi, lived in Melbourne. Her closest boy chum, Andy, had just moved with his family to England.

Partly for these reasons, her overall media time budget probably remained unchanged.

She clung to the landline like a drowning teenager to a life raft. After school, she'd install herself in the family room, echoey and airplane-hangar-like now that it had been clear-felled of its media and their bulky accoutrements, and hold court before an unseen audience for two or three hours at a clip. She assured me that both Maddi and Andy had their parents' permission to ring her as often as they liked; it seems they had magic Internet landlines that made long- distance calls for free, "Or just about."

"What if you need to ring them?" I wanted to know.

"Easy. I just send them a signal—I ring once or twice and then hang up. Really, Mum, we've got it all figured out."

Many people have asked me if there was ever a moment during the electronic media blackout when I was tempted to quit. Not counting April 25, the day I received a phone bill for $1,123.26, I can honestly say, no. Not at all.

Digital Immigrants use technology to achieve specific ends. Digital Natives breathe technology in order to ... well, breathe. To exist. Before, Sussy had pretty much lived online. Now she was pretty much living on the phone. Cleverly, she also used it to gain access to banned media. "Google 'Nick Jonas!'" she'd bark into the phone to Maddi, when the need to know the details of Miley Cyrus' relationship status grew unbearably urgent, or, "Check my Facebook!" (the girls regularly, and companionably, hacked each others' accounts anyhow), or, "Message Andy and tell him to ring me at eight my time." Maddi was now more than a best friend. She was Sussy's personal remote outsourcer, carrying out her digital bidding with terrifying dispatch.

Their relationship changed in less obvious ways, too, during those marathon conversations, and so did her connection with Andy. "On MSN, you're kind of almost waving at people. You get introduced, and it's like hi and LOL and ILY and stuff ... but you never really get to know them," she explained to me. "On the phone, it's totally different. It's like D&M [deep and meaningful] You get close. You get tight."

I Tweet, Therefore I Am

PEGGY ORENSTEIN

On a recent lazy Saturday morning, my daughter and I lolled on a blanket in our front yard, snacking on apricots, listening to a download of E. B. White reading "The Trumpet of the Swan." Her legs sprawled across mine; the grass tickled our ankles. It was the quintessential summer moment, and a year ago, I would have been fully present for it. But instead, a part of my consciousness had split off and was observing the scene from the outside: this was, I realized excitedly, the perfect opportunity for a tweet.

I came late to Twitter. I might have skipped the phenomenon altogether, but I have a book coming out this winter, and publishers, scrambling to promote 360,000-character tomes in a 140-character world, push authors to rally their "tweeps" to the cause. Leaving aside the question of whether that actually boosts sales, I felt pressure to produce. I quickly mastered the Twitterati's unnatural self-consciousness: processing my experience instantaneously, packaging life as I lived it. I learned to be "on" all the time, whether standing behind that woman at the supermarket who sneaked three extra items into the express check-out lane (you know who you are) or despairing over human rights abuses against women in Guatemala.

Each Twitter post seemed a tacit referendum on who I am, or at least who I believe myself to be. The grocery-store episode telegraphed that I was tuned in to the Seinfeldian absurdities of life; my concern about women's victimization, however sincere, signaled that I also have a soul. Together they suggest someone who is at once cynical and compassionate, petty yet deep. Which, in the end, I'd say, is pretty accurate.

Distilling my personality provided surprising focus, making me feel stripped to my essence. It forced me, for instance, to pinpoint the dominant feeling as I sat outside with my daughter listening to E.B. White.

Was it my joy at being a mother? Nostalgia for my own childhood sum-
mers? The pleasures of listening to the author's quirky, underinflected
voice? Each put a different spin on the occasion, of who I was within it.
Yet the final decision ("Listening to E.B. White's 'Trumpet of the Swan'
with Daisy. Slow and sweet.") was not really about my own impressions: it
was about how I imagined—and wanted—others to react to them. That
gave me pause. How much, I began to wonder, was I shaping my Twitter
feed, and how much was Twitter shaping me?

Back in the 1950s, the sociologist Erving Goffman famously argued
that all of life is performance: we act out a role in every interaction, adapting it based on the nature of the relationship or context at hand. Twitter
has extended that metaphor to include aspects of our experience that used
to be considered off-set: eating pizza in bed, reading a book in the tub,
thinking a thought anywhere, flossing. Effectively, it makes the grease-
paint permanent, blurring the lines not only between public and private
but also between the authentic and contrived self. If all the world was
once a stage, it has now become a reality TV show: we mere players are
not just aware of the camera; we mug for it.

The expansion of our digital universe—Second Life, Facebook, MyS-
pace, Twitter—has shifted not only how we spend our time but also how
we construct identity. For her coming book, "Alone Together," Sherry
Turkle, a professor at M.I.T., interviewed more than 400 children and
parents about their use of social media and cellphones. Among young
people especially she found that the self was increasingly becoming exter-
nally manufactured rather than internally developed: a series of profiles to
be sculptured and refined in response to public opinion. "On Twitter or
Facebook you're trying to express something real about who you are," she
explained. "But because you're also creating something for others' consumption, you find yourself imagining and playing to your audience more
and more. So those moments in which you're supposed to be showing
your true self become a performance. Your *psychology* becomes a performance." Referring to "The Lonely Crowd," the landmark description of
the transformation of the American character from inner- to outer-di-
rected, Turkle added, "Twitter is outer-directedness cubed."

The fun of Twitter and, I suspect, its draw for millions of people, is
its infinite potential for connection, as well as its opportunity for self-ex-
pression. I enjoy those things myself. But when every thought is exter-
nalized, what becomes of insight? When we reflexively post each feeling,
what becomes of reflection? When friends become fans, what happens

to intimacy? The risk of the performance culture, of the packaged self, is that it erodes the very relationships it purports to create, and alienates us from our own humanity. Consider the fate of empathy: in an analysis of 72 studies performed on nearly 14,000 college students between 1979 and 2009, researchers at the Institute for Social Research at the University of Michigan found a drop in that trait, with the sharpest decline occurring since 2000. Social media may not have instigated that trend, but by encouraging self-promotion over self-awareness, they may well be accelerating it.

None of this makes me want to cancel my Twitter account. It's too late for that anyway: I'm already hooked. Besides, I appreciate good writing whatever the form: some "tweeple" are as deft as haiku masters at their craft. I am experimenting with the art of the well-placed "hashtag" myself (the symbol that adds your post on a particular topic, like #ShirleySherrod, to a stream. You can also use them whimsically, as in, "I am pretending not to be afraid of the humongous spider on the bed. #lieswetellourchildren").

At the same time, I am trying to gain some perspective on the perpetual performer's self-consciousness. That involves trying to sort out the line between person and persona, the public and private self. It also means that the next time I find myself lying on the grass, stringing daisy chains and listening to E. B. White, I will resist the urge to trumpet about the swan.

The Myth of Multitasking

CHRISTINE ROSEN

In one of the many letters he wrote to his son in the 1740s, Lord Chesterfield offered the following advice: "There is time enough for everything in the course of the day, if you do but one thing at once, but there is not time enough in the year, if you will do two things at a time." To Chesterfield, singular focus was not merely a practical way to structure one's time; it was a mark of intelligence. "This steady and undissipated attention to one object, is a sure mark of a superior genius; as hurry, bustle, and agitation, are the never-failing symptoms of a weak and frivolous mind."

In modern times, hurry, bustle, and agitation have become a regular way of life for many people—so much so that we have embraced a word to describe our efforts to respond to the many pressing demands on our time: *multitasking.* Used for decades to describe the parallel processing abilities of computers, multitasking is now shorthand for the human attempt to do simultaneously as many things as possible, as quickly as possible, preferably marshalling the power of as many technologies as possible.

In the late 1990s and early 2000s, one sensed a kind of exuberance about the possibilities of multitasking. Advertisements for new electronic gadgets—particularly the first generation of handheld digital devices—celebrated the notion of using technology to accomplish several things at once. The word multitasking began appearing in the "skills" sections of résumés, as office workers restyled themselves as high-tech, high-performing team players. "We have always multitasked—inability to walk and chew gum is a time-honored cause for derision—but never so intensely or self-consciously as now," James Gleick wrote in his 1999 book *Faster.* "We are multitasking connoisseurs—experts in crowding, pressing, packing, and overlapping distinct activities in our all-too-finite moments." An arti-

Christine Rosen is a senior editor of The New Atlantis *and a fellow at the Ethics and Public Policy Center.*

Rosen, Christine. "The Myth of Multitasking." *The New Atlantis* 20 (Spring 2008): n.p. Web. 16 Mar. 2011. <http://www.thenewatlantis.com/publications/the-myth-of-multitasking>. ©The New Atlantis.

cle in the *New York Times Magazine* in 2001 asked, "Who can remember life before multitasking? These days we all do it." The article offered advice on "How to Multitask" with suggestions about giving your brain's "multitasking hot spot" an appropriate workout.

But more recently, challenges to the ethos of multitasking have begun to emerge. Numerous studies have shown the sometimes-fatal danger of using cell phones and other electronic devices while driving, for example, and several states have now made that particular form of multitasking illegal. In the business world, where concerns about time-management are perennial, warnings about workplace distractions spawned by a multitasking culture are on the rise. In 2005, the BBC reported on a research study, funded by Hewlett-Packard and conducted by the Institute of Psychiatry at the University of London, that found, "Workers distracted by e-mail and phone calls suffer a fall in IQ more than twice that found in marijuana smokers." The psychologist who led the study called this new "infomania" a serious threat to workplace productivity. One of the Harvard *Business Review's* "Breakthrough Ideas" for 2007 was Linda Stone's notion of "continuous partial attention," which might be understood as a subspecies of multitasking: using mobile computing power and the Internet, we are "constantly scanning for opportunities and staying on top of contacts, events, and activities in an effort to miss nothing."

Dr. Edward Hallowell, a Massachusetts-based psychiatrist who specializes in the treatment of attention deficit/hyperactivity disorder and has written a book with the self-explanatory title *CrazyBusy,* has been offering therapies to combat extreme multitasking for years; in his book he calls multitasking a "mythical activity in which people believe they can perform two or more tasks simultaneously." In a 2005 article, he described a new condition, "Attention Deficit Trait," which he claims is rampant in the business world. ADT is "purely a response to the hyperkinetic environment in which we live," writes Hallowell, and its hallmark symptoms mimic those of ADD. "Never in history has the human brain been asked to track so many data points," Hallowell argues, and this challenge "can be controlled only by creatively engineering one's environment and one's emotional and physical health." Limiting multitasking is essential. Best-selling business advice author Timothy Ferriss also extols the virtues of "single-tasking" in his book, *The 4-Hour Workweek.*

Multitasking might also be taking a toll on the economy. One study by researchers at the University of California at Irvine monitored interruptions among office workers; they found that workers took an average of twenty-five minutes to recover from interruptions such as phone calls or answering e-mail and return to their original task. Discussing multitasking with the *New York Times* in 2007, Jonathan B. Spira, an analyst at the business research firm Basex, estimated that extreme multitasking—information overload—costs the U.S. economy $650 billion a year in lost productivity.

CHANGING OUR BRAINS

To better understand the multitasking phenomenon, neurologists and psychologists have studied the workings of the brain. In 1999, Jordan Grafman, chief of cognitive neuroscience at the National Institute of Neurological Disorders and Stroke (part of the National Institutes of Health), used functional magnetic resonance imaging (fMRI) scans to determine that when people engage in "task-switching"—that is, multitasking behavior—the flow of blood increases to a region of the frontal cortex called Brodmann area 10. (The flow of blood to particular regions of the brain is taken as a proxy indication of activity in those regions.) "This is presumably the last part of the brain to evolve, the most mysterious and exciting part," Grafman told the *New York Times* in 2001—adding, with a touch of hyperbole, "It's what makes us most human."

It is also what makes multitasking a poor long-term strategy for learning. Other studies, such as those performed by psychologist René Marois of Vanderbilt University, have used fMRI to demonstrate the brain's response to handling multiple tasks. Marois found evidence of a "response selection bottleneck" that occurs when the brain is forced to respond to several stimuli at once. As a result, task-switching leads to time lost as the brain determines which task to perform. Psychologist David Meyer at the University of Michigan believes that rather than a bottleneck in the brain, a process of "adaptive executive control" takes place, which "schedules task processes appropriately to obey instructions about their relative priorities and serial order," as he described to the *New Scientist*. Unlike many other researchers who study multitasking, Meyer is optimistic that, with training, the brain can learn to task-switch more effectively, and there is some evidence that certain simple tasks are amenable to such practice. But his research has also found that multitasking contributes to the release of stress hormones and adrenaline, which can cause long-term health problems if not controlled, and contributes to the loss of short-term memory.

In one recent study, Russell Poldrack, a psychology professor at the University of California, Los Angeles, found that "multitasking adversely affects how you learn. Even if you learn while multitasking, that learning is less flexible and more specialized, so you cannot retrieve the information as easily." His research demonstrates that people use different areas of the brain for learning and storing new information when they are distracted: brain scans of people who are distracted or multitasking show activity in the striatum, a region of the brain involved in learning new skills; brain scans of people who are not distracted show activity in the hippocampus, a region involved in storing and recalling information. Discussing his research on National Public Radio recently, Poldrack warned, "We have to be aware that there is a cost to the way that our society is changing, that humans are not built to work this way. We're really built to focus. And when we sort of force ourselves to multitask, we're driving ourselves to perhaps be less efficient in the long run even though it sometimes feels like we're being more efficient."

If, as Poldrack concluded, "multitasking changes the way people learn," what might this mean for today's children and teens, raised with an excess of new entertainment and educational technology, and avidly multitasking at a young age? Poldrack calls this the "million-dollar question." Media multitasking—that is, the simultaneous use of several different media, such as television, the Internet, video games, text messages, telephones, and e-mail—is clearly on the rise, as a 2006 report from the Kaiser Family Foundation showed: in 1999, only 16 percent of the time people spent using any of those media was spent on multiple media at once; by 2005, 26 percent of media time was spent multitasking. "I multitask every single second I am online," confessed one study participant. "At this very moment I am watching TV, checking my e-mail every two minutes, reading a newsgroup about who shot JFK, burning some music to a CD, and writing this message."

The Kaiser report noted several factors that increase the likelihood of media multitasking, including "having a computer and being able to see a television from it." Also, "sensation-seeking" personality types are more likely to multitask, as are those living in "a highly TV-oriented household." The picture that emerges of these pubescent multitasking mavens is of a generation of great technical facility and intelligence but of extreme impatience, unsatisfied with slowness and uncomfortable with silence: "I get bored if it's not all going at once, because everything has gaps—waiting for a website to come up, commercials on TV, etc." one participant said. The report concludes on a very peculiar note, perhaps intended to be optimistic: "In this media-heavy world, it is likely that brains that are more adept at media multitasking will be passed along and these changes will be naturally selected," the report states. "After all, information is power, and if one can process more information all at once, perhaps one can be more powerful." This is techno-social Darwinism, nature red in pixel and claw.

Other experts aren't so sure. As neurologist Jordan Grafman told *Time* magazine: "Kids that are instant messaging while doing homework, playing games online and watching TV, I predict, aren't going to do well in the long run." "I think this generation of kids is guinea pigs," educational psychologist Jane Healy told the *San Francisco Chronicle*; she worries that they might become adults who engage in "very quick but very shallow thinking." Or, as the novelist Walter Kirn suggests in a deft essay in *The Atlantic,* we might be headed for an "Attention-Deficit Recession."

PAYING ATTENTION

When we talk about multitasking, we are really talking about attention: the art of paying attention, the ability to shift our attention, and, more broadly, to exercise judgment about what objects are worthy of our attention. People who have achieved great things often credit for their success a finely honed skill for paying attention. When asked about his particular genius, Isaac Newton responded that if he had made any discoveries, it was "owing more to patient attention than to any other talent."

William James, the great psychologist, wrote at length about the varieties of human attention. In *The Principles of Psychology* (1890), he outlined the differences among "sensorial attention," "intellectual attention," "passive attention," and the like, and noted the "gray chaotic indiscriminateness" of the minds of people who were incapable of paying attention. James compared our stream of thought to a river, and his observations presaged the cognitive "bottlenecks" described later by neurologists: "On the whole easy simple flowing predominates in it, the drift of things is with the pull of gravity, and effortless attention is the rule," he wrote. "But at intervals an obstruction, a set-back, a log-jam occurs, stops the current, creates an eddy, and makes things temporarily move the other way."

To James, steady attention was thus the default condition of a mature mind, an ordinary state undone only by perturbation. To readers a century later, that placid portrayal may seem alien—as though depicting a bygone world. Instead, today's multitasking adult may find something more familiar in James's description of the youthful mind: an "extreme mobility of the attention" that "makes the child seem to belong less to himself than to every object which happens to catch his notice." For some people, James noted, this challenge is never overcome; such people only get their work done "in the interstices of their mind-wandering." Like Chesterfield, James believed that the transition from youthful distraction to mature attention was in large part the result of personal mastery and discipline—and so was illustrative of character. "The faculty of voluntarily bringing back a wandering attention, over and over again," he wrote, "is the very root of judgment, character, and will."

Today, our collective will to pay attention seems fairly weak. We require advice books to teach us how to avoid distraction. In the not-too-distant future we may even employ new devices to help us overcome the unintended attention deficits created by today's gadgets. As one *New York Times* article recently suggested, "Further research could help create clever technology, like sensors or smart software that workers could instruct with their preferences and priorities to serve as a high tech 'time nanny' to ease the modern multitasker's plight." Perhaps we will all accept as a matter of course a computer governor—like the devices placed on engines so that people can't drive cars beyond a certain speed. Our technological governors might prompt us with reminders to set mental limits when we try to do too much, too quickly, all at once.

Then again, perhaps we will simply adjust and come to accept what James called "acquired inattention." E-mails pouring in, cell phones ringing, televisions blaring, podcasts streaming—all this may become background noise, like the "din of a foundry or factory" that James observed workers could scarcely avoid at first, but which eventually became just another part of their daily routine. For the younger generation of multi-taskers, the great electronic din is an expected part of everyday life. And given what neuroscience and anecdotal evidence have shown us, this state of constant intentional self-distraction could well be of profound detriment to individual and cultural well-being. When people do their work only in the "interstices of their mind-wandering," with crumbs of attention rationed out among many competing tasks, their culture may gain in information, but it will surely weaken in wisdom.

Spotify Doesn't Hurt Artists: My Band Would Be Nowhere Without It

BEN BERRY

Spotify has been the topic of much debate the past few weeks, thanks in part to Taylor Swift's decision to pull her catalog from the service and Aloe Blacc's op-ed here on WIRED entitled "Streaming Services Need to Pay Songwriters Fairly."

I have a different point of view. For my young band Moke Hill, which I formed with my friend Andrew Phillips in 2013, Spotify hasn't been a negative, but an enormous positive.

We laid the foundation for Moke Hill with an EP that came out at the end of 2013, then worked on new material to complete a full-length release as a basis to secure label, management and booking partners. Over the course of this year, with no marketing, PR or label support, Spotify has exposed those songs to an audience who would otherwise have little chance of finding us. At last check, our song "Detroit" has been streamed 310,187 times.

Before switching over to the artist's side of things, I spent several years on the business end of the industry, working at an indie label and management company. That experience gave me exposure to the process of how revenue flows from consumers to artists, and how that process is changing with new technology.

NUMBERS TELL THE STORY BEST

To prove how good Spotify has been for us, I dug into the value of streaming payments using the data available to me: Moke Hill Spotify numbers.

Ben Berry is an independent musician, songwriter and member of the band Moke Hill.

Berry, Ben. "Spotify Doesn't Hurt Artists: My Band Would Be Nowhere Without It." *Wired*. Conde Nast Digital, 24 Nov. 2014. <http://www.wired.com/2014/11/one-band-who-loves-spotify>. © Conde Nast Publications, Inc.

Here are the payment numbers reported to date for "Detroit" (the payments haven't caught up with the actual streams yet):

204,250 Spotify streams = $910.43

This means we're getting paid approximately 0.4457 cents for every stream. Since we didn't/don't have a label, we used a distribution service to get the EP to the digital services and never pressed any physical copies. That service takes 15 percent off the top, so Spotify is actually paying out more than we're seeing (approx. 0.5244 cents/stream).

The math won't be exact, but applying our per stream numbers to the Avicii song "Wake Me Up" that Aloe Blacc references in his article tells me that Spotify will pay out upwards of $1,563,792 on the streams for that song, to date. I reach that number by multiplying our cents per stream by 298,203,998 current plays and dividing by $0.85, since our distribution service takes 15 percent. So that's over $1.5 million for one song, on one still relatively small streaming service.

That doesn't sound so bad, right? It might even make you wonder why everyone is so upset with Spotify. The answer is complex, but the revenue generated from Spotify streams is divided much the same way it is on iTunes, and CD sales before that.

Here's how Spotify revenue breaks down. Spotify keeps approximately 30 percent of the gross revenue, which they use to pay employees and keep the service running (major labels have an approximately 20 percent ownership share in Spotify, which is included in that 30 percent). Approximately 60 percent is paid out to the owner of the masters (usually labels but in Moke Hill's case, us, through our distribution company) and approximately 10 percent to the owner of the publishing.

UNDERSTANDING THE TERMS OF A DEAL

The biggest issue with most of the arguments against Spotify is that we don't know the terms of the artists' contracts. What are the details of their label deal? Do the songwriters have a publishing deal? Did the songwriter get an advance on his publishing deal? What is the songwriter's split on the song(s) they wrote? Without any of this information, we can't tell exactly what is happening to the money after Spotify writes the check.

It isn't Spotify's fault that the money isn't making its way to the artists. These artists sign deals with publishing companies and labels to get the protection, distribution, expertise and exposure that come along with them. There is a huge advantage in having a label behind you, but that advantage comes at a cost. Let's not blame Spotify because a label or publishing company is taking a cut of what Spotify pays, based on the terms of whatever deal they made with the individual artists. Spotify simply adheres to the model that has been in place for years, and therefore pays roughly the same percentage of revenue to master owners/publishers as CDs or iTunes.

In Taylor Swift's case, we don't know exactly why she decided to pull her catalog, but last week her label president (Scott Borchetta) made this comment:

"If [a] fan went and purchased the record, CD, iTunes, wherever, and then their friends go, 'why did you pay for it? It's free on Spotify,' we're being completely disrespectful to that superfan."

I'm not sure I follow his logic, but I do know that the music is not "free" on Spotify, since many users (myself included) are paying for the service, and the rest are paying in the form of ads. I might go so far as to say that it's "disrespectful" (to use his word) to force fans to buy CDs or use iTunes when they likely left that model years ago (or never joined it in the first place, in the case of many younger consumers).

The music industry failed to find a reasonable solution when CD burning and piracy took off, choosing instead to try and force fans to buy CDs. Why? Because half a century ago labels realized that they could make more money by forcing consumers to buy a full album instead of the individual songs they actually wanted, and labels today haven't had the desire to innovate and change a system that was working to their benefit. We now have a sustainable model that can re-invigorate recorded music, and the industry is still fighting it in an effort to push people back to CDs and iTunes.

Rather than fighting, I believe the industry should embrace the change that's coming (or more accurately, the change that has already arrived). Technological advances have made mobile access to millions of songs a reality—this is a great thing for music fans. Subscribers paying for the mobile version of Spotify in the US are spending ~$120 per year on the service—well above (almost 5x by some reports) what the average music listener spends on music per year. More people spending more money on recorded music (since Spotify's total revenue increases with each new user) leads to bigger payouts for artists, writers, labels and publishing companies alike.

Meanwhile, there's another issue that's been under the radar of the Spotify debate: artists now make the majority of their money on the road. This increase was the industry's response to the dramatic fall in revenue from album sales, meaning that fans are still paying for music and supporting artists—just in a different way. Taylor Swift made nearly $40 million dollars last year—approximately $30 million (or ¾ of her income) from touring. Swift stated in *Time* that she "think(s) there should be an inherent value placed on art." I couldn't agree more. And obviously, so do her fans; in a year that she didn't release a record, she made $40 million dollars. Sounds like "inherent value" to me.

Further confusing the issue, Swift's label president told *Time*, "Taylor Swift has been paid less than $500,000 in the past 12 months for domestic streaming of her songs."

That number is deceptive, considering the $500k referenced includes US streams only, in a 12 month period that began a full year after she released her last album, "Red". In other words, it's not surprising that her streams and sales would be down when she hadn't put out a record in a year. Borchetta is also using a number that only accounts for approximately 30 percent of Spotify's total paying users.

It's pretty safe to assume that Taylor Swift's numbers for this year would have blown these out of the water, considering her first week (1.2 million album sales) was the largest sales week for an album since 2002. "Shake It Off" was streamed 46.3 million times on Spotify in October before it was pulled.

LET'S NOT OVERSIMPLIFY

I have nothing but respect for Taylor Swift and Aloe Blacc and any musician trying to do this for a living, but I hope artists will pause and realize that misplaced blame and oversimplification of the issues could set us back. Physical album sales are not the long-term solution (case in point: the laptop I'm typing on doesn't have a CD drive), and the alternative to streaming is piracy or YouTube (which has historically paid poorly, and allows users to upload anything they want, resulting in artists getting nothing for many of the streams).

Spotify is in it's infancy, so the payout numbers are much smaller now than they will be as the service grows. Imagine if Spotify were embraced by notable musicians and revenue grew to 10 times what it is today (and the streams per song along with it); the singles mentioned above could be generating $9 to $17 million dollars each—for one song.

As for Moke Hill, we've spent next to nothing to get our songs on Spotify and it has exposed us to tens of thousands of people around the world who never would have heard our music otherwise. Spotify is not only paying us, but building our fan base while paying us, which will eventually make it easier to sell tickets to shows.

I worry that if more big acts follow Taylor Swift's lead, bands like ours could lose an important outlet to have their music heard. And I can say definitively that were it not for Spotify, I would never have discovered many of the artists I consider favorites today.

#TheDress and the Rise of Attention-Policing

MEGAN GARBER

It caused Taylor Swift to feel "confused and scared." It caused a rupture in the Kardashian-West household that might never be repaired. It caused Chris Murphy, a Democratic representative from Connecticut, to come out and say, "I know three things: 1) the ACA works; 2) climate change is real; 2) [sic] that dress is gold and white." It caused the rest of us to question our sanity and our friends and the nature of reality.

The basic problem with The Dress—having gone viral on *BuzzFeed* last night, it has already come to stand in for all dresses, Platonically—is this: Some people see it as blue and black. Others see it as white and gold. And each side is, like, 1,000 percent sure that they see the dress as it is, in reality—so sure that the conversations about the dress have tended to play out as ALL-CAPS ASSERTIONS OF OBJECTIVE TRUTH because OMG YOU GUYS IT'S WHITE AND GOLD AND IF YOU CAN'T SEE THAT THEN I DON'T EVEN KNOW WHAT TO TELL YOU. (And also as ALL-CAPS DEC-LARATIONS of a slightly more mod-est variety: "I swear to you its no hoax," Swiked, who wrote the Tumblr post that launched a thousand existential doubts, promised. "I saw the dress in real life, it's blue and black. Some peo-ple just see this pic as white and gold. I DONT HAVE ANY ANSWERS BUT I NEED THEM.")

Here is what The Dress, as depicted across the Internet, looks like:

Garber, Megan. "#TheDress and the Rise of Attention-Policing." *The Atlantic*. The Atlantic Monthly Group, 27 Feb. 2015. Web. 2 Apr. 2015. <http://m.theatlantic.com/technology/archive/2015/02/thedress-and-the-rise-of-attention-policing/386357/>. © Atlantic Media, Inc.

The visual/moral/existential discrepancies—*ceci n'est pas une robe*—are most likely traceable to the play of light on the pigment rhodopsin, found in the rods of the human eye, and also to the glorious dynamism of the human sensory experience, though maybe also to a hoax of Santa and/or Söze proportions, and possibly also to a rupture in the space-time continuum that can be mended only by Matthew McConaughey's dimples. Regardless. The Rorschach dress—the dress that, as so many news outlets have reminded us, has "broken the Internet"—has brought us together; it has divided us; it has caused us to question the physical world and our place within it and hinted that perception is relative and also that while facts may be sacred they are also uncomfortably unsteady. Maybe the left shark was actually yellow, and what is yellow anyway, I mean like how would you describe yellow to a blind person, and have you ever really looked at your hand, like really looked, and HOW CAN YOU NOT SEE WHAT I SEE and maybe The Matrix was onto something and I AM SORRY BUT IT IS SO OBVIOUSLY WHITE AND GOLD and either way we will all die alone.

So, yeah. You can read the dress—sorry, #thedress—as a metaphor: for our knee-jerk impulse toward partisanship (#TEAMBLUEAND-BLACK), for the dynamic nature of observable reality (#TEAM-WHITEANDGOLD), for the Internet's ability to prove Walt Whitman right yet again, for its ability to prove Daniel Patrick Moynihan wrong yet again, for the fundamental challenge of consensus-building in American democracy, for Plato's caves and Russell's turtles and Bill Murray's groundhog. What I want to focus on, though, is a little sliver of all that: a particular strain of commentary that arose during the explosion of conversation about #thedress. Here is a representative tweet, from God (well, @TheTweetofGod) himself:

This is a line of logic that will be familiar from most any Meme Event—the logic that says, basically, "don't look at that; that is unimportant." It's attention-policing, and it's reminiscent of so many other strains of rhetorical legislation that play out in online conversations: *You can't say that. You can't talk about that.* GUYS, the attention-policer usually begins. How can you be talking about *a dress/a leg/a pair of llamas/a dancing neoprene shark* when *climate change/net neutrality/marriage equality/ISIS/China/North Korea* is going on?

The world, to be sure, is a complicated and often tragic and often deeply unfair place. It contains famines and genocides and war, births and deaths, Katy Perry and Björk, Big Macs and kale and Bloomin' Onions, privilege and the lack of it, llamas that are caged and llamas that are free. And we humans—animals who are striving to be so much more—have a big say in the balance between the good and the bad. We should not be glib about any of that. Nor should we lose sight of the fact that, if you find yourself with the ability to use the most transformational communications platform the world has ever known to engage in debates about the color of a dress being sold on Amazon.com, you are, fundamentally, extremely privileged. And thus in a better position than most to make the world better. Attention is a valuable thing; we have an obligation to be selective about where we direct it.

And yet. The problem with attention-policing—besides the fact that it tends to be accompanied by humorlessness and marmery, and besides the other fact that it serves mostly to amplify the ego of the person doing the policing—is that it undermines the value of Internet memes themselves. Those memes, whether they involve #thedress or #llamadrama or #leftshark or #whathaveyou, are culturally lubricating. They create, and reinforce, the imagined community. Last night, we needed each other— not just to share and joke and laugh, but also to prove to ourselves that we weren't going completely crazy. "TELL ME WHAT COLOR THIS DRESS IS," I texted a friend. "OKAY, PHEW," I texted again, when he saw it as white-and-gold. I also, on the other hand, mock-disowned a significant percentage of the people I love in a haze of #whiteandgold partisanship—but even that kind of faux-fighting has its value. Theorists of play, from Huizinga to Piaget, have pointed out how powerful the infrastructures of games can be. They allow us to explore ideas and bond in a mutually-agreed-upon environment. Jane McGonigal, the game designer and theorist, suggests that the alternate universes provided by video games allow us to think in terms of collaboration and problem-solving. Games' constraints, she argues, are actually empowering.

And what are memes if not games? They are small; they are low-stakes; they are often silly. (Sorry, #llamadrama.) But they are also communal. They invite us to participate, to adapt, to joke, to create something together, under the auspices of the same basic rules. That is not a small thing. That is, in fact, a huge thing—particularly when it comes to the very concerns the attention police like to remind us of. If we have any hope of solving the world's most systemic and sweeping problems, we will have to come together. Inequality, climate change, injustices both enormous and less so ... these will require cooperative action. They will require us to collaborate and compromise and value diversity. The dress makes a pretty good metaphor for all that. Also, it is totally white and gold.

Welcome to the New Reputation Economy

RACHEL BOTSMAN

Imagine a world where banks take into account your online reputation alongside traditional credit ratings to determine your loan; where headhunters hire you based on the expertise you've demonstrated on online forums such as Quora; where your status from renting a house through Airbnb helps you become a trusted car renter on WhipCar; where your feedback on eBay can be used to get a head-start selling on Etsy; where traditional business cards are replaced by profiles of your digital trustworthiness, updated in real-time. Where reputation data becomes the window into how we behave, what motivates us, how our peers view us and ultimately whether we can or can't be trusted.

Welcome to the reputation economy, where your online history becomes more powerful than your credit history.

The value of reputation is not a new concept to the online world: think star ratings on Amazon, PowerSellers on eBay or reputation levels on games such as *World of Warcraft*. The difference today is our ability to capture data from across an array of digital services. With every trade we make, comment we leave, person we "friend", spammer we flag or badge we earn, we leave a trail of how well we can or can't be trusted.

An aggregated online reputation having a real-world value holds enormous potential for sectors where trust is fractured: banking; e-commerce, where value is exponentially increased by knowing who someone really is; peer-to-peer marketplaces, where a high degree of trust is required between strangers; and where a traditional approach based on disjointed information sources is currently inefficient, such as recruiting.

Joel Spolsky and Jeff Atwood, programmers and influential blog-

Rachel Botsman is social innovator, writer and speaker who is writing a book on reputation capital. She wrote about conscientious consumption in 03.12

Botsman, Rachel. "Welcome to the New Reputation Economy." *Wired*. Wired UK., 20 Aug. 2012. Web. 26 Mar. 2015. <http://www.wired.co.uk/magazine/archive/2012/09/features/welcome-to-the-new-reputation-economy>. © Conde Nast Publications, Inc.

gers, saw the window of opportunity to reinvent the way people found jobs through online reputation a few years ago. "Traditional wikis and Q&A platforms drove me crazy," Atwood says. If you had questions, say, on Chrome extensions, double pointers or Tiny Pixels, "you had to wade through endless conversations that went in every possible direction and where no comment is more or less important than the previous one. We realised there was a need to optimise the way people got answers, to unearth the little gems buried among a lot of dreck." The way to solve this seemed obvious to Atwood. "Have people vote on the best answers, and rank answers," he says.

In September 2008, Atwood and Spolsky launched Stack Overflow. A sort of Digg meets Wikipedia meets eBay, it is a platform for programmers to post detailed technical questions and receive answers from other programmers. "As soon as I touched it, I was hooked," says Marc Gravell, a 33-year-old user based near the Forest of Dean, who, with more than 315,000 points, has the site's second-highest reputation score. Stack Overflow reports more than 24 million unique visitors a month and around 5,500 questions are submitted to the site every day.

Voting on and editing questions are just two ways in which users can earn reputation points on Stack Overflow. "Reputation is earned by convincing your peers that you know what you are talking about," Spolsky says. "The reason why the site is 100 percent spam-free and that around 80 percent of all questions get answered is entirely a function of the community. The way we do that is as you earn more reputation points, you get more powers on the site."

Shortly after the site launched, Atwood and Spolsky heard that programmers were putting their Stack Overflow reputation scores on their CVs, and headhunters were searching the platform for developers with specific skills. "A CV tells you what schools they went to, what companies they worked for and how well they did on a standardised test when they were teenagers," Spolsky explains. "But if you read the writings of someone on Stack Overflow, you immediately know if they are a skilled programmer or not." In February 2011, Stack Overflow launched Careers 2.0, an invitation-only job board where companies can find skilled programmers.

Stack Overflow demonstrates how a person's reputation score created in one community is starting to have value beyond the environments where it was built. By answering questions in an expert forum, you create more opportunities to find a better job.

Reputation information can also be used to look forward rather than back—for instance, using past actions to work out the likelihood of someone honouring an agreement in the future, which could be particularly useful in the financial services industry. "Any kind of business based on credit has to take into account people's ability to repay and their propensity to pay," says Errol Damelin, founder of Wonga, the online short-term cash lender (Wired 06.11). "Even when they are able to repay, will they or won't they? It's a totally different question. That's when reputation really comes into play." Wonga claims to crunch on average 8,000 pieces of data to get a sense of how trustworthy its applicants are.

Brett King, author of *Bank 2.0* and founder of New York-based banking startup Movenbank, founded in 2010, agrees with Damelin. "Credit scores are a lagging indicator—they only look at what has happened in the past," he says. "They [credit agencies] don't use data to look into whether your behaviour is risky or not now."

Movenbank's goal is not just to use technology to personalise the banking experience, but to reinvent the traditional risk model. King spent more than 18 years working for traditional banks and was struck by the opacity of much of the credit assessment process. "Most banks reject around 50 per cent of credit applications. It's a pretty strange business when you reject half of your potential customers and don't even tell them why."

At the heart of Movenbank is a concept call CRED. This takes into account an individual's traditional credit score but also aspects such as their level of community involvement, social reputation and trust weighting. Do they have a good eBay rating? Do they send money peer-to-peer? It also measures their social connectivity—how many friends do they have on Facebook? Who are they connected to on LinkedIn? Do they have an influential Klout score? It combines this data, not just to assess their risk, but to measure the potential value of the customer. If you refer other customers from your network or pay your bills on time, your CRED score will go up. "It's not about your credit, but your credibility," King says.

A big question mark lies around people's readiness to open up their social data, but King believes consumers are willing to make a trade-off if they know how it is going to be used and what they will gain in return. "People are currently underusing their networks and reputation," King says. "I want to help people to understand and build their influence and reputation, and think of it as capital they can put to good use."

Social scientists have long been trying to quantify the value of reputation. In 2008, Norihiro Sadato, a researcher at the National Institute for Physiological Sciences in Aichi, Japan, along with a team of colleagues, wanted to determine whether we think about reputation and money in the same way, by mapping the neural response to different rewards. "Although we all intuitively know that a good reputation makes us feel good, the idea that good reputation is a reward has long been just an assumption in social sciences," Sadato says. "There has been no scientific proof."

In order to prove his hypothesis, Sadato devised an experiment: participants were told they were playing a simple gambling game, in which one of three cards would result in a cash payout. Using functional magnetic resonance imaging, the researchers monitored brain activity triggered when the subjects received a monetary reward. When the subjects returned on the second day, they were each shown a picture of their face, with a one-word descriptor underneath that a panel of strangers had supposedly written about them. Some of the descriptions were positive, such as "trustworthy", others neutral, such as "patient", and others negative. When participants heard they had a positive reputation, a part of the brain, the striatum, lit up.

The same part would also light up if they had won money. As Sadato puts it: "The implication of our study is that different types of reward are coded by the same currency system." In other words, our brains neurologically compute personal reputation to be as valuable as money.

Personal reputation has been a means of making socioeconomic decisions for thousands of years. The difference today is that network technologies are digitally enabling the trust we used to experience face-to-face—meaning that interactions and exchanges are taking place between total strangers.

Trust and reputation become acutely important in peer-to-peer marketplaces such as WhipCar and Airbnb, where members are taking a risk renting out their cars or their homes. The difference between these community-driven marketplaces and e-commerce sites is that they are connecting real people with real names in the offline world. When you are trading peer-to-peer, you can't count on traditional credit scores. A different measurement is needed. Reputation fills this gap because it's the ultimate output of how much a community trusts you.

"Reputation allows you to bring over some of the history of who you are as a person, whether it's in the digital or the real world," says Brian Chesky, cofounder and CEO of Airbnb, the peer-to-peer marketplace that matches people with space to rent with those looking for accommodation. "What has surprised me the most about reputation is that the need for it actually goes down as the marketplace matures."

In other words, a host's or a guest's reputation gets users comfortable with trusting the idea (staying in or renting the homes of complete strangers), trusting the system (Airbnb) and trusting the recipient. "By the time a host has their 20th guest on Airbnb, they start blindly accepting people. They don't need to talk on the phone or need lots of information," he explains. "You start trusting people. So really what we are doing is not just renting out spaces but helping to change the way people trust humanity."

Chesky is aware of the value of the data users are building on Airbnb. "The platforms that will become the centrepiece of online reputation are the ones that create some kind of meaningful relationships, and carry the data on defining who you really are as a person," says the 30-year-old. He believes, however, that Airbnb has a trust currency that is "super interesting for others because the transactions are in person and not just online. We capture data about people's real-world behaviours that could not be captured on any other website."

But this wealth of data raises an important question—who owns our reputation? Shouldn't our hard-earned online status be portable? If you're a SuperHost on Airbnb, shouldn't you be able to use that reputation to, say, get a loan, or start selling on Etsy? "I know we are creating a really important currency that could be useful outside of Airbnb," Chesky says.

Presently, reputation data doesn't transfer between verticals. Consequently, if a host has a high rating on Airbnb, but no reputation on a competitor's platform, they can feel locked in. "I imagine that people will leverage their Airbnb reputation in ways that we can't yet imagine," Chesky says. "Airbnb could become a story of your life and that story should be able to follow you." A wave of startups, including Connect.Me, TrustCloud, TrustRank, Legit and WhyTrusted, are trying to solve this problem by designing systems that correlate reputation data. By building a system based on "reputation API"—a combination of a user's activity, ratings and reviews across sites—Legit is working to build a service that gives users a score from zero to 100. In trying to create a universal metric for a person's trustworthiness, they are trying to "become the credit system of the sharing economy", says Jeremy Barton, the 27-year-old San Francisco-based cofounder of Legit.

His company, and other reputation ventures, face some big challenges if they are to become, effectively, the PayPal of trust. The most obvious is coming up with algorithms that can't be easily gamed or polluted by trolls. And then there's the critical hurdle of convincing online marketplaces not just to open up their reputation vaults, but create a standardised format for how they frame and collect reputation data. "We think companies will share reputation data for the same reasons banks give credit data to credit bureaux," says Rob Boyle, Legit cofounder and CTO. "It is beneficial for one company to give up their slice of reputation data if in return they get access to the bigger picture: aggregated data from other companies."

When asked for the sources upon which a user's trustworthiness is based, reputation startups list the usual suspects—LinkedIn, Facebook, Twitter—but refuse to go further, saying that the algorithm is proprietary. For these trust-validation services to become credible they're going to need to differentiate their products from those offered by companies such as PeerIndex, Kred and Klout, which collect digital information from different social-media sources. Their metrics—who I "follow", who "follows" me, who I know professionally, where I check in, what I chat about—are measuring social influence, not reputation. "Influence measures your ability to drag someone into action," says Joe Fernandez, cofounder of San Francisco-based Klout (wired 08.12). "Reputation is an indicator of whether a person is good or bad and, ultimately, are they trustworthy?"

Influence aggregators are trailblazers for the bigger reputation economy. Yes, it's easy to point out that a Klout score is merely a popularity contest, but what the likes of Klout and PeerIndex are starting to show is that it's possible to extract value from the information exchanged by groups across networks. "Think about people on social media," says Azeem Azhar, the 39-year-old founder of PeerIndex. "They are spending around 500 minutes a month investing time on their networks. It's like they are building a living CV across their lives, so it makes it important for them to get value out of that."

Early influence and reputation aggregators will undoubtedly learn by trial and error—but they will also face the significant challenge of pioneering the use of reputation data in a responsible way. And there's a challenge beyond that: reputation is largely contextual, so it's tricky to transport it to other situations. Sure, you might be an impeccable Airbnb host, but does that mean I would trust you with my car? "When you build reputation in a specific system," explains Coye Cheshire, an associate professor at the UC Berkeley School of Information, whose work focuses on trust dynamics in online interactions, "it must be seen in light of the social dynamics, the population and the unique characteristics of that system."

Many of the ventures starting to make strides in the reputation economy are measuring different dimensions of reputation. On Stack Overflow, for instance, reputation is a measure of knowledge; on Airbnb it's a measure of trust; on Wonga it's a measure of propensity to pay; on Klout and PeerIndex it's a measure of influence.

Reputation capital is not about combining a selection of different measures into a single number—people are too nuanced and complex to be distilled into single digits or binary ratings.

It's the culmination of many layers of reputation you build in different places that genuinely reflect who you are as a person and figuring out exactly how that carries value in a variety of contexts.

The most basic level is verification of your true identity—is this person a real person? Are they who they say they are? It's also foreseeable that data giving a good indicator of character, such as reliability and helpfulness, in one marketplace is a baseline of how you will behave in another marketplace. Do we do what we say we are going to do? How well do we respect another person's property? Can we be trusted to pay on time? But the big, sticky area around porting reputation lies in the space of shared interests, values and connections that can be pulled from the social graph. Currently platforms such as Airbnb are only using this data to connect a person with some kind of mutual connection, such as going to the same university. The larger opportunity is carrying social matches based on like-minded individuals across marketplaces.

These multifaceted sources of reputation will not be a single algorithm: we will be able to perform a Google- or Facebook-like search and see a picture of a person's behaviour in many different contexts, over a length of time. Slivers of data that have until now lived in secluded isolation online will be available in one place. Answers on Quora, reviews on TripAdvisor, comments on Amazon, feedback on Airbnb, videos posted on YouTube, social groups joined, or presentations on SlideShare; as well as a history and real-time stream of who has trusted you, when, where and why. The whole package will come together in your personal reputation dashboard, painting a comprehensive, definitive picture of your intentions, capabilities and values.

"We are only at day one in the whole idea of global reputation," Chesky says. "There really could one day be this reputation economy that allows us to do so many different activities that we can't even imagine right now."

By the end of the decade, a good online reputation could be the most valuable currency in your possession.

THE NEW IDENTITY BROKERS

A raft of services have been founded over the past year, all promising to monitor and police your online reputation.

Connect.Me

Aims to turn your social profile into a personal reputation network, making it easier to find trustworthy people, from accountants to babysitters. (In beta.)

Tru.ly

Enables users to verify their digital identity against their real-world one by authenticating social profile data against official government data.

Legit

Correlates reputation data from a number of P2P marketplaces into a "LegitScore" and a report that summarises user behaviours. (In beta.)

TrustCloud

Aggregates public data and correlates it into a "TrustScore" that measures online behaviour. Its aim: to let you own your online trustworthiness.

Scaffold

Builds easy-to-use APIs and tools that enable P2P marketplaces to conduct background checks and verify a user's identity and reputation.

Confido

Wants to become the "FICO of social commerce" by providing a portable profile that users can carry across P2P marketplaces. (In beta.)

Briiefly

Working on combining indicators from across social networks and offline activities to create a trust profile and score. (In beta.)

Reputate

Aims to create a snapshot of a person's online reputation by aggregating reviews and ratings across P2P marketplaces. (In beta.)

THE TEN-STEP REPUTATION PLAN

Want to be a trusted member of the online community? Follow these tips on building your reputation capital.

Be a maven

Demonstrate your knowledge on something—music, maths, movies—on MavenSay, Mahalo or StackExchange.

Get tagging

Use a platform such as Skills.to to tag your strengths and make it easy for others to know at a glance what you can do.

Become super at something

Be a great host, runner, seller, renter, lender, in an online marketplace such as Airbnb, WhipCar or Zopa.

Build a portfolio

Make a note of references, ratings and reviews on various platforms that give a snapshot of your online value.

Collect trusted opinions

Ask people who know and trust you to write about your skills and trustworthiness on platforms such as LinkedIn.

Follow, like, befriend

Concentrate on building a deep social network on at least one platform. Interact, follow and "like" on a daily basis.

Review and recommend

Get your name out there: be active in writing reviews and vouching for friends and colleagues on a range of websites.

Monetise your profile

Build some kind of virtual currency account, whether it's Linden Dollars, Gold Coins, IMVU or Facebook Credits.

Spring clean your reputation

Use a service such as Reputation.com or Veribo to clean up any misleading or false information about you.

Gain some social capital

Become an active part of your local community and demonstrate you are trustworthy in your personal life.

Bibliography

SPIRITUAL PERSPECTIVES

Ballard, M. Russell. "Sharing the Gospel Using the Internet." Commencement address at BYU-Hawaii, December 2007. *Ensign.* July 2008. Web. 5 April 2011.

Bednar, David A. "Things as They Really Are." CES Fireside for Young Adults. Rexburg, Idaho. 3 May 2009.

Bednar, David A. "To Sweep the Earth as with a Flood." Education Week. BYU. 19 August 2014.

EDUCATION

Bauerlein, Mark. "Online Literacy Is a Lesser Kind." *The Chronicle Review.* 19 Sept. 2008. Web. 12 Mar. 2011.

Burton, Gideon. "Dear Students: Don't Let College Unplug Your Future." *Academic Evolution.* 6 Jan 2009.

Selsberg, Andy. "Teaching to the Text Message." *The New York Times.* 19 March 2011. Web. 21 March 2011.

Turkle, Sherry. "How Computers Change the Way We Think." *Chronicle of Higher Education.* 30 Jan. 2004. EBSCO. Web. 14 Mar. 2011.

Keim, Brandon. "Why the Smart Reading Device of the Future May Be . . . Paper." *Wired.* 1 May 2014. <http://www.wired.com/2014/05/reading-on-screen-versus-paper/>.

Weise, Michelle. "The Real Revolution in Online Education Isn't MOOCs." *Harvard Business Review.* Harvard Business Publishing, 17 Oct. 2014. Web. <http://blogs.hbr.org/2014/10/the-real-revolution-in-online-education-isnt-moocs/>.

Bruff, Derek. "A Social Network Can Be a Learning Network." *The Chronicle of Higher Education.* 6 Nov. 2011. <http://chronicle.com/article/A-Social-Network-Can-Be-a/129609/>.

Singer, Natasha. "They Loved Your G.P.A. Then They Saw Your Tweets." *The New York Times.* The New York Times Company. 9 Nov. 2013. <http://www.nytimes.com/2013/11/10/business/they-loved-your-gpa-then-they-saw-your-tweets.html?pagewanted=all&_r=0>.

Cullinane, Mary. "Why Free Is Not the Future of Digital Content in Education." *Wired.com*. Wired., 25 Mar. 2015. Web. 26 Mar. 2015. <http://www.wired.com/2015/03/free-not-future-digital-content-education/>.

Lapowsky, Issie. "Why Free Online Classes Are Still the Future of Education." *Wired*. 26 Sept. 2014. <http://www.wired.com/2014/09/free-online-classes-still-future-education/>.

POLITICS

Carr, Nicholas. "Is Google Making us Stupid?" *The Atlantic*. July/August 2008. Web. 12 March 2011.

Gladwell, Malcolm. "The Revolution Will Not Be Tweeted." *The New Yorker*. 4 Oct 2010. Web. 13 March 2011.

Lee, Edward. "Why Malcolm Gladwell Should Apologize to Social Media." *Huffington Post*. HuffingtonPost.Com, Inc. 13 Feb. 2011. <http://www.huffingtonpost.com/edward-lee/why-malcolm-gladwell-shou_b_822640.html>.

Shirky, Clay. "The Political Power of Social Media." *Foreign Affairs* 90.1 (Jan/Feb 2011): n.p. EBSCO. Web. 14 March 2011.

Fisher, Shannon. "Why 'Slacktivism' Matters." *MediaShift*. 25 Feb 2015.

Robertson, Charlotte. "Slacktivism: The Downfall of Millennials." *Huffington Post*. 14 Oct 2014. http://www.huffingtonpost.com/charlotte-robertson/slacktivism-the-downfall-_b_5984336.html

RELATIONSHIPS

Lynn, Regina. "Don't Dismiss Online Relationships as Fantasy." *Wired* 7 Sept. 2007. Web. 12 Mar. 2011. <http://www.wired.com/culture/lifestyle/commentary/sexdrive/2007/09/sexdrive_0907>.

Lynn, Regina. "Rude People, Not Tech, Cause Bad Manners." *Wired* 21 Sept. 2007. Web. 12 Mar. 2011. <http://www.wired.com/culture/lifestyle/commentary/sexdrive/2007/09/sexdrive_0921>.

Manjoo, Farhad. "You Have No Friends." *Slate*. 14 Jan. 2009. Web. 12 Mar. 2011. <http://www.slate.com/id/2208678>.

McArthur, Micah. "Are We Facebook Friends Yet?" *The Universe*. 2 Dec. 2009. Web. 12 Mar. 2011. <http://www.universe.byu.edu/node/4570>.

Allard, Jody. "Why I Don't Watch What My Kids are Doing Online." *Free Range Kids*. 27 Aug. 2014. <http://www.freerangekids.com/why-i-dont-watch-what-my-kids-are-doing-online/>.

Bennett, Jessica. "Bubbles Carry a Lot of Weight." *The New York Times*. 24 Aug. 2014. <http://www.nytimes.com/2014/08/31/fashion/texting-anxiety-caused-by-little-bubbles.html?_r=0>.

Lucsombe, Belinda. "This Is How to Stalk Your Teenage Children Online." *Time.* Time, Inc. 20 Oct. 2014. <http://time.com/3523213/men-women-and-children-internet-safety-kids/>.

Pierson, Emma. "Re: Our Relationship." *The Atlantic.* The Atlantic Monthly Group, 31 Mar. 2015. Web. 2 Apr. 2015. <http://www.theatlantic.com/technology/archive/2015/03/re-our-relationship/389030/>.

DIGITAL CULTURE

Carr, Nicholas. "The Amorality of Web 2.0." *Rough Type.* Blog post. 3 Oct. 2005. Web. 12 Mar. 2011.

Rosen, Jay. "The People Formerly Known as the Audience." Blog Post. *PressThink.* 27 June 2006. Web. 13 Mar. 2011. <http://archive.pressthink.org/2006/06/27/ppl_frmr.html>.

Maushart, Susan. "When My Kids Unplugged." *Salon.* 22 Jan. 2011. Web. 17 Mar. 2011. <http://www.salon.com/life/feature/2011/01/22/winter_of_disconnect/index.html>.

Orenstein, Peggy. "I Tweet, Therefore I Am." *The New York Times Magazine.* 30 July 2010. Web. 14 Mar. 2011. <http://www.nytimes.com/2010/08/01/magazine/01wwln-lede-t.html>.

Rosen, Christine. "The Myth of Multitasking." *The New Atlantis* 20 (Spring 2008): n.p. Web. 16 Mar. 2011. <http://www.thenewatlantis.com/publications/the-myth-of-multitasking>.

Berry, Ben. "Spotify Doesn't Hurt Artists: My Band Would Be Nowhere Without It." *Wired.* Conde Nast Digital, 24 Nov. 2014. <http://www.wired.com/2014/11/one-band-who-loves-spotify>.

Garber, Megan. "#TheDress and the Rise of Attention-Policing." *The Atlantic.* The Atlantic Monthly Group, 27 Feb. 2015. Web. 2 Apr. 2015. http://m.theatlantic.com/technology/archive/2015/02/thedress-and-the-rise-of-attention-policing/386357/>.

Botsman, Rachel. "Welcome to the New Reputation Economy." *Wired.* Wired UK., 20 Aug. 2012. Web. 26 Mar. 2015. <http://www.wired.co.uk/magazine/archive/2012/09/features/welcome-to-the-new-reputation-economy>.